AMIENS 1918

The Black Day of the German Army

CAMPAIGN • 197

AMIENS 1918

The Black Day of the German Army

ALISTAIR McCLUSKEY   ILLUSTRATED BY PETER DENNIS

Series editors Marcus Cowper and Nikolai Bogdanovic

First published in Great Britain in 2008 by Osprey Publishing,
Midland House, West Way, Botley, Oxford OX2 0PH, UK
443 Park Avenue South, New York, NY 10016, USA
E-mail: info@ospreypublishing.com

A CIP catalogue record for this book is available from the British Library

ISBN: 978 1 84603 303 2

Editorial by Ilios Publishing Ltd, Oxford, UK (www.iliospublishing.com)
Page layout by: The Black Spot
Index by Alison Worthington
Typeset in Sabon and Myriad Pro
Maps by The Map Studio Ltd
3D bird's-eye views by The Black Spot
Battlescene illustrations by Peter Dennis
Originated by PDQ Digital Media Solutions
Printed in China through Worldprint Ltd.

08 09 10 11 12   10 9 8 7 6 5 4 3 2 1

FOR A CATALOGUE OF ALL BOOKS PUBLISHED BY OSPREY MILITARY
AND AVIATION PLEASE CONTACT:

NORTH AMERICA
Osprey Direct, c/o Random House Distribution Center, 400 Hahn Road,
Westminster, MD 21157
E-mail: info@ospreydirect.com

ALL OTHER REGIONS
Osprey Direct UK, P.O. Box 140 Wellingborough, Northants, NN8 2FA, UK
E-mail: info@ospreydirect.co.uk

Osprey Publishing is supporting the Woodland Trust, the UK's leading
woodland conservation charity, by funding the dedication of trees.

www.ospreypublishing.com

ACKNOWLEDGMENTS

This book is the result of two years of work and could not have happened
without the help of the following people; Dr Peter Lieb of the War Studies
Department, and Mr Andrew Orgill and his Library team, both of the Royal
Military Academy Sandhurst; Peter Dennis for bringing ideas to life; Marcus
and Nikolai at Ilios for understanding missed deadlines; Yvonne Oliver of
the Imperial War Museum Photographic Department and all the staff of
Osprey Publishing. The encouragement, advice and assistance has been
essential in guiding my thoughts; however, any errors that remain are my
own. As a serving soldier I am acutely aware that the story told is built on
the endurance and sacrifice of the soldiers and airmen of all nations that
took part in the battle of Amiens. I would ask that all readers keep them
in mind as they use this book.

In addition to the material support provided by those mentioned
above, the project would have been impossible without the love and
understanding of my family, in particular Sue and Ben who for too long
endured a husband and father absorbed in a forgotten battle when he
should have been providing romantic dinners, drawing dinosaurs and
making Lego pirate ships.

IMPERIAL WAR MUSEUM COLLECTIONS

Some of the photos in this book come from the Imperial War Museum's
huge collections which cover all aspects of conflict involving Britain
and the Commonwealth since the start of the twentieth century.
These rich resources are available online to search, browse and buy at
www.iwmcollections.org.uk. In addition to Collections Online, you can
visit the Visitor Rooms where you can explore over 8 million photographs,
thousands of hours of moving images, the largest sound archive of its
kind in the world, thousands of diaries and letters written by people in
wartime, and a huge reference library. To make an appointment, call
(020) 7416 5320, or e-mail mail@iwm.org.uk.

Imperial War Museum www.iwm.org.uk

ARTIST'S NOTE

Readers may care to note that the original paintings from which the
colour plates in this book were prepared are available for private sale.
The Publishers retain all reproduction copyright whatsoever. All enquiries
should be addressed to:

Peter Dennis, The Park, Mansfield, Notts, NG18 2AT

The Publishers regret that they can enter into no correspondence upon
this matter.

Key to military symbols

CONTENTS

Western Front, July 1918, Foch's strategic plan

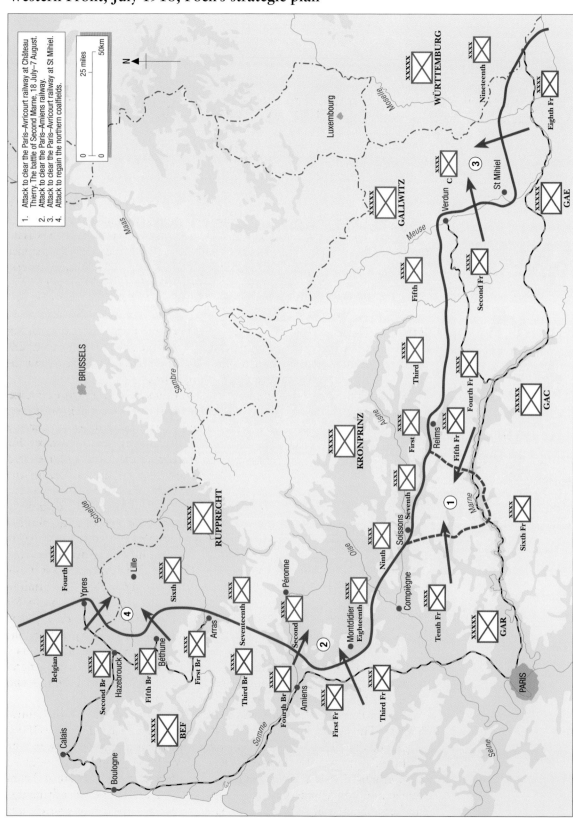

1. Attack to clear the Paris–Avricourt railway at Château Thierry. The battle of Second Marne, 18 July–7 August.
2. Attack to clear the Paris–Amiens railway.
3. Attack to clear the Paris–Avricourt railway at St Mihiel.
4. Attack to regain the northern coalfields.

25 miles

50km

N

Luxembourg

WÜRTTEMBURG

Nineteenth

Eighth Fr

GALLWITZ

Verdun

St Mihiel

GAE

Meuse

Fifth

Second Fr

Third

Fourth Fr

BRUSSELS

Sambre

Maas

KRONPRINZ

Aisne

First

Reims

Fifth Fr

GAC

RUPPRECHT

Soissons

Seventh

Marne

Schelde

Fourth

Lille

Sixth

Péronne

Oise

Ninth

Compiègne

Sixth Fr

Ypres

Belgian

Second Br

Hazebrouck

Fifth Br

Béthune

First Br

Arras

Third Br

Seventeenth

Second

Montdidier

Eighteenth

Tenth Fr

GAR

PARIS

Calais

Boulogne

BEF

Fourth Br

Amiens

First Fr

Third Fr

Somme

Seine

1

2

3

4

ORIGINS OF THE CAMPAIGN

The battle of Amiens was one of the most important and influential engagements fought in World War I. Although in terms of Allied casualties per day it was no less bloody than the attritional assaults launched in 1916 and 1917, the manner in which it was fought shattered the German Second and Eighteenth armies, and clearly demonstrated that the German Army was a beaten force in the field. Despite the fact that the Germans fought hard after Amiens, the sophisticated operational and tactical techniques utilized by the British Fourth and French First armies highlighted the Allied ability to achieve success almost at will in either positional or open warfare. As such it was arguably the high watermark of Allied combat performance in World War I and heralded a mode of combat that would characterize warfare in the 20th century.

Although the battle delivered spectacular results from four days of intense combat, the overall outcome was fundamentally shaped by the fighting during the preceding months during which time the conditions were set for the Franco-British attack. The first six months of 1918 had been disastrous for the Allies. Militarily weak and politically fractured, they faced a rejuvenated German Army that drove them to the brink of defeat. Following the harrowing battles of 1917, the British, French and Italian armies spent the winter attempting to recuperate their combat strength with dwindling manpower reserves, whilst American troops arrived in France at a painfully slow rate. In order to cope with their manpower shortage, the British Army followed the French lead and reduced the strength of their divisions from 12 to nine infantry battalions, disbanding 115 battalions in the process. Only the Canadian and Australian divisions were able to retain their 12-battalion structure. Political differences added to the problems they faced. Authority for the strategic conduct of the war was uncertain as the newly formed Supreme War Council at Versailles chafed against the national military aspirations of the individual Allies. In January, attempts by the Supreme War Council to divert forces from the West to Italy and Palestine, and to form a general reserve on the Western Front were resisted by Pétain and Haig, who maintained that their armies were too weak to give up troops.

The weakness of the Allies was seen as a vital opportunity by the Central Powers. The German high command, the Oberste Heeresleitung (OHL), concluded that defeat would be inevitable once the American Army was fully deployed in late 1918. However, Russia's collapse in late 1917 released 42 German divisions that could be transferred to the Western Front immediately, giving the German Army a short-term manpower advantage. Furthermore, new attack doctrines characterized by surprise, massive artillery

The Kaiser, with Hindenburg (left) and Ludendorff (right). The German high command denuded the front at Amiens as they attempted to husband their forces for a decisive assault in Flanders. (IWM Q 23746)

bombardments over a short period of time and deep infiltration by specially trained 'stormtroop' (*Stosstruppe*) infantry units had been proved at Riga and Cambrai in late 1917, suggesting that the trench deadlock may be coming to an end. Consequently, Hindenburg and Ludendorff resolved to bring the Allies to the peace table before the American influence could be felt by defeating the Allied armies in France with a series of massive assaults.

The German offensive was launched on 21 March on an 80km front from Arras to La Fère. Spearheaded by an artillery bombardment from 6,500 guns, 74 divisions of the German Second, Seventeenth and Eighteenth armies smashed into the 30 divisions of the British Third and Fifth armies. Operation *Michael* drove the British back 65km in eight days and briefly threatened to separate them from the French to the south. However, the exhausted German assault troops were halted by British and French reserves assembled in front of the key rail centre of Amiens, forming a front line that remained relatively static until August.

The German attack brought the factional infighting between the Allies to an end. On 26 March at a conference in Doullens, The Supreme War Council appointed Foch as generalissimo on the Western Front in operational command of both the British and French armies. This move brought much needed coherence to the Allied effort as they were tested by further German offensives in France and Belgium. Operation *Mars* saw the Seventeenth Army unsuccessfully attempt to extend the gains of *Michael* towards Arras. Operation *Georgette* pushed the British First and Second armies back 16km in the valley of the river Lys between 9 and 27 April.

May brought a pause to the offensives whilst the Germans re-oriented their assault to the south in an attempt to draw the Allied reserves away from the decisive sector in the north. Operation *Goerz* was launched on 27 May between Reims and Soissons. A deep salient was again driven into the Allied line with a subsidiary attack being launched on the river Matz between 9 and 13 June. The final German assault opened on 15 July at Reims. After a limited gain in ground it was halted by a massive counterattack three days later spearheaded by the French Tenth Army, which reclaimed the territory lost since 27 May.

The Marne counterattack caused Ludendorff to postpone what he hoped would be the decisive assault in Flanders, Operation *Hagen*. However, he did not consider that the strategic initiative had passed irrevocably to the Allies.

Whilst the German offensives were taking place in the late spring and summer, the conditions for the battle of Amiens were being set on the Somme. Between April and July, the Australian Corps occupied the Amiens sector of the front as part of Rawlinson's Fourth Army. During this period they had developed a doctrine of aggressive patrolling they called 'peaceful penetration'. This concept used fighting patrols to attack the isolated outposts of the German defensive positions who were thinly spread to avoid Allied artillery strikes. A fearful toll was exacted as small groups 'vanished' from the battlefield as Australian prisoners. Furthermore, the Australians reported that little attempt was being made to construct defences by the German Second Army and that morale seemed to be low. Testing the weakness of the Germans before him, Rawlinson mounted an attack at Hamel on 4 July when the 4th Australian Division, supported by 60 tanks, captured 1,500 German troops in their forward positions. Sensing the opportunity to repeat the attack but on a much larger scale, Rawlinson proposed an attack east of Amiens to Haig on 5 July. Rawlinson was directed to draft a more detailed plan although Haig still wanted to see Rupprecht's strategic reserves drawn into battle elsewhere before he moved onto the offensive.

Rawlinson's plans were developed concurrently with a new strategic approach that Foch outlined in a directive issued on 24 July. Firstly, he wished to secure his ability to manoeuvre troops around the Western Front by driving the Germans away from the Paris–Avricourt and Paris–Amiens railways. Secondly, he wished to regain the lost coal-mining area in the north and drive the enemy back from Calais and Dunkirk. Haig began to bring the concepts together on 26 July when he recommended Rawlinson's plan to the generalissimo. Foch agreed in principle, but insisted that the attack be mounted jointly with the French First Army under Général Debeney, with the whole operation being commanded by Haig. Haig agreed and 10 August was set as the date of the attack. However, throughout this period Foch's overriding concern was to maintain the pressure on the Germans in the wake of the Marne counterattack, and on 3 August he persuaded Haig to advance the Amiens attack to 8 August.

CHRONOLOGY

21 March Operation *Michael* commences.

5 April Operation *Michael* finishes with the front line on Santerre and the Avre Valley east of Amiens.

20 May Foch memorandum proposes assault between the Oise and Somme to free the Amiens–Paris railway.

4 July Battle of Hamel.

14 July Fourth Army instructed to prepare assault at Amiens by GHQ.

17 July Rawlinson's first plan submitted to Haig with 10 August as provisional attack date.

23 July Haig gives general approval to Rawlinson's plan.

24 July Bombon Château Conference. Foch outlines his strategic plan for Western Front. Approval given to Amiens plan with proviso that French First Army included.

28 July Foch advances date of attack to 8 August.

29 July Objectives extended to include Roye and Chaulnes.

6 August 27th Division assault on Morlancourt Ridge.

8 August

0420hrs III, Australian and Canadian corps launch attack.

0505hrs French First Army commences attack.

0820hrs Assault on second objective commences. French IX Corps launches attack at Genonville and La Neuville.

1100hrs Australian and Cavalry corps commence attack on the third objective.

1130hrs 5th Australian Division is the first infantry formation to occupy the third objective.

1200hrs RAF begin attacks on the Somme bridges.

1430hrs Gruppen Gutscher and Lägeler launch counterattack south of Morlancourt.

1700hrs 2nd Canadian Division is the last formation to occupy the third objective.

2230hrs French XXXI Corps secures Fresnoy-en-Chaussée.

9 August

0430hrs 11th Canadian Brigade attacks Le Quesnel.

0800hrs	French XXXI Corps attacks Hangest.	2130hrs	Australian Corps attacks at Proyart and Etinehem.
0900hrs	221st and 79th reserve divisions deploy at Arvillers and Folies. 38th Division deploys at Chaulnes.	**11 August**	
		0400hrs	Australian Corps seizes Lihons.
1200–1300hrs	German III Corps counterattacks French XXXI Corps around Hangest.	0420hrs	French XXXI Corps recommences attack towards Roye.
1600hrs	French XXXIV Corps attacks south of Montdidier.	0845hrs	German XI Corps counterattacks at Lihons and Crépey Wood.
1615hrs	British III Corps recommences attack north of the Somme.	1000hrs	I Bavarian Corps counterattacks at Hallu.
2200hrs	German III Corps ordered to withdraw to l'Echelle–Conchy Line. I Bavarian Corps promised to Eighteenth Army.	1630hrs	Final attack by German XI Corps.
		2200hrs	Haig and Foch agree to halt operations on Amiens front bringing the battle of Amiens to a conclusion.
10 August			
0420hrs	8th Canadian Brigade attacks Le Quesnoy. French Third Army launches assault south-east of Montdidier.	**21 August**	Battle of Albert.
		22 August	Battle of the Scarpe.
0430hrs	French XXXI Corps attacks towards Roye.	**1 September**	Fourth Army cross the Somme at Péronne.
0730hrs	French XXXIV Corps recommences attack towards Roye.	**26 September**	General offensive commences with Franco-American battle of the Argonne.
0800hrs	Australian Corps recommences attack towards Lihons. Canadian Corps recommence attack towards Roye.	**27 September**	Battle of the Canal du Nord.
1000hrs	60th Division occupies Montdidier.	**28 September**	Battle of Ypres 1918.
1100hrs	Haig meets with Foch and agrees to continue advance. British Third Army ordered to commence operations towards Bapaume.	**29 September**	Fourth Army breaks the Hindenburg Line.
1130hrs	IX and III brigades RAF attack Péronne railway station. Heavy fighting with JGs I and II.	**17 October**	Battle of the Selle.
		1 November	Battle of Valenciennes
1530hrs	Cavalry Corps launches unsuccessful attack towards Roye and Nesle.	**4 November**	Battle of the Sambre.
1730hrs	5th Bavarian Division counterattacks at Crépey Wood.	**11 November**	Germany signs the Armistice.

OPPOSING COMMANDERS

ALLIED COMMANDERS

Maréchal Ferdinand Foch was an artilleryman who had combat command experience at corps, army and army group level by the end of 1915. Foch became Chief of the French General Staff in mid-1917 and generalissimo from that post. During this time he developed his strategic concept of a series of sequenced attacks in different sectors, as an alternative to the breakthrough that had eluded his predecessors. He was an aggressive, energetic optimist who constantly drove subordinate commanders forwards. However, he also possessed a flexible mind when circumstances demanded and was not afraid to accept their advice when necessary.

Field Marshal Sir Douglas Haig commanded the BEF. Haig was a cavalryman who began the war as a corps commander. Given command of the First Army at the end of 1914, he succeeded Sir John French as commander of the BEF after the battle of Loos in late 1915. He led the BEF through the testing Somme, Arras and Passchendaele campaigns of 1916–17, during which time he oversaw its transition to a 'citizen army' on the Continental scale. Haig took a close interest in developments in the military profession

The Allied commanders together with King George V after the battle. Rawlinson stands to the left on the front row followed from left to right by Debeney, Foch, King George and Haig. (IWM Q 9250)

Lieutenant-General Sir John Monash and the staff of the Australian Corps. Behind Monash from left to right are brigadier-generals C. H. Foott (engineers), R. A. Carruthers (DA and QMG), T. A. Blamey (chief of staff), L. D. Fraser, (heavy artillery) and W. A. Coxen (artillery). (IWM E(Aus) 2750)

throughout his career. Contrary to his postwar reputation as being stubborn and conservative in his approach, he fully encouraged the exploitation of emerging aircraft and tank technologies in his armies and by 1918 had developed more effective relationships with his army commanders.

For the battle of Amiens, Haig was given control of the French First Army alongside his own Fourth Army. For the battle of Amiens the Fourth Army consisted of the III, Australian, Canadian, Cavalry and Tank corps and was commanded by **General Sir Henry Rawlinson**. Rawlinson was an experienced leader, having commanded a division and a corps through the battles of 1914–15. Promoted to command of Fourth Army in 1916 his performance at the battle of the Somme was poor. He repeatedly lacked the confidence to back his own judgement against that of Haig. The Fourth Army staff was 'sidelined' during 1917, and Rawlinson moved to the Supreme War Council in 1918. He replaced Gough in command of Fifth Army at the end of Operation *Michael* and successfully defended Amiens. The Fifth Army was then 'renamed' as Fourth Army and remained in Picardy for the spring and summer.

Lieutenant-General Sir Richard Butler commanded III Corps. Butler was a protégé of Haig and had served as a staff officer in I Corps, First Army and HQ BEF. During his time with the BEF he irritated senior army commanders, Rawlinson included, by his offhand treatment of them. His experience in command was limited. He moved to III Corps in January 1918 taking a part in the defence against Operation *Michael*. **Lieutenant-General Sir John Monash** commanded the Australian Corps. Monash was a civil engineer by profession and had been a member of the prewar Militia. He joined the AIF in 1914 and served in Gallipoli as a brigade commander and on the Western

Front as a divisional commander until his promotion to corps command in June 1918. Monash insisted that the operations of the Australian Corps were thoroughly prepared and he had a reputation as being cool under pressure, a clear communicator and a quick learner. His counterpart in the Canadian Corps was **Lieutenant-General Sir Arthur Currie.** Currie was also a member of the prewar Militia, during which time he almost destroyed his military career through dubious financial dealings. He mobilized in 1914 and commanded a brigade at the battle of Second Ypres, and a division at the battles of the Somme and Arras. He was promoted to command of the Canadian Corps for the battle of Third Ypres. Like Monash, he also planned his operations with great care, maximizing the use of firepower whenever he could. **Lieutenant-General Sir Charles Kavanagh** commanded the Cavalry Corps. Since September 1916 Kavanagh had had the unenviable task of turning a 'break in' into a 'breakthrough'. Participation in the successful defensive battles of First and Second Ypres, as commander of a cavalry brigade and subsequently a cavalry division, had illustrated the difficulties presented by obstacles and firepower to mounted troops. He proved adept at using dismounted cavalry in support of infantry but showed caution when moving his corps into the vanguard of an assault, taking care to maintain the support of infantry and artillery where possible.

Général **Eugène Debeney** commanded the French First Army. Debeney began the War as Chief of Staff First Army. In May 1915 he became GOC 25th Infantry Division and saw combat in the early stages on the battle of Verdun. He was promoted to corps command in April 1916 and led XXXII Corps at the Somme. He was promoted to army command in December 1916 and became GOC First Army in December 1917. He took part in the defensive battles that halted the *Michael* offensive between Montdidier and Amiens in March 1918, where his performance was methodical rather than mercurial as he took care to avoid overextending the troops under his command.

Général **Paul-Louis Toulorge** commanded XXXI Corps. Toulorge spent the period between January 1916 and February 1918 in command of the 130th and then 27th infantry divisions. He saw extensive action at Verdun in 1916 and was promoted to command of XXXI Corps in February 1918, with which he took part in the battles around Villers-Brettoneux in April. **Général Noël-Marie Garnier-Duplessis** commanded IX Corps. Garnier-Duplessis commanded the 37th Infantry Division between October 1916 and June 1918. He saw combat at Verdun in 1916 and during the Nivelle Offensive in 1917. He took over command of IX Corps in June 1918. X Corps was commanded by **Général Charles Vandenburg,** who had experience as a divisional commander between October 1914 and March 1917 during which time he took part in the battle of the Somme. He took over command of X Corps in March 1917. **Général Charles Jacquot** commanded XXXV Corps. Jacquot was a highly experienced combat leader having commanded the 6th

The HQ of 3rd Canadian Division in the field at Amiens. This image vividly illustrates the attempts to operate effective command and control in 1918 at the tactical level. Staff and dispatch riders wait in the background to distribute orders and receive reports of the battle situation. (IWM CO 2981)

Division at the Aisne in 1914, the battles of Second and Third Artois in 1915 and the battle of Verdun in 1916. He was promoted to command XXXV Corps in April 1916 and saw further combat on the Somme in 1916 and against the *Michael* offensive in 1918. II Cavalry Corps was commanded by **Général Félix Robillot**, but played little part in the battle.

The French Third Army played a peripheral role in the battle and was commanded by **Général Georges Humbert**. It consisted of XXXIV Corps, commanded by **Général Alphonse Nudant**, and XV Corps commanded by **Général Jacques de Riols de Fonclare**.

GERMAN COMMANDERS

The German Second and Eighteenth armies were part of Heeresgruppe Rupprecht, commanded by **Kronprinz Rupprecht of Bavaria**. Rupprecht was a professional soldier who commanded the Sixth Army in Lorraine and Flanders in 1914–15. Given command of the most northerly German army group, he demonstrated a dogged determination in defence during 1916–17 at the battles of the Somme, Arras and Third Ypres.

General Georg von der Marwitz was commander of the Second Army. He led a cavalry group on the Western Front in 1914 before moving to command a corps at the battle of the Masurian Lakes on the Eastern Front in 1915. He took over the Second Army in 1916 and first experienced the new British attack doctrines at Cambrai in 1917. He mounted a partially successful counterattack at Cambrai using the 'infiltration' tactics perfected in the East, and his army was at the centre of the *Michael* offensive. However, he was unable to capture Amiens and the main effort was moved to Hutier's Eighteenth Army.

Generalleutnant Alfred von Larisch commanded LIV Corps. Larisch commanded the 10th, 81st Reserve and Guard Ersatz divisions between February 1915 and January 1918. He had combat experience at Verdun in 1916 and Riga in 1917. In January 1918 he took over command of the LIV Corps, which he led during Operation *Goerz* in May and June before moving north to take over the Württemburg divisions between Albert and the Somme. South of the Somme **Generalleutnant Viktor Kühne** commanded XI Corps. Kühne commanded 25th Infantry Division from August 1914 to September 1916 on the Western and Eastern fronts where he served under Marwitz. He saw combat at Gorlice-Tarnow and Verdun before promotion to corps command in November 1917. He commanded XI Corps during Operation *Michael*. On the left flank of Second Army was **Generalleutnant Eberhard von Hofacker's** LI Corps. Hofacker had experience in command of both cavalry and infantry divisions on both the Western and Eastern fronts. He took part in the defensive battles in Flanders in 1917 before being promoted to command LI Corps in October 1917, which he led through Operation *Michael*.

General Oskar von Hutier commanded the Eighteenth Army. Hutier commanded 1st Guards Infantry Division until April 1915 with whom he fought on the Marne. He commanded XXI Corps from April 1915 to January 1917. In April 1917 he took command of the Eighth Army on the Eastern Front where he gained a formidable reputation for his exploitation of infantry

Kronprinz Rupprecht of Bavaria. Despite his success in the defensive battles of 1916–17, Rupprecht and his staff spent the period between May and July 1918 focussed on the development of the proposed *Hagen* offensive around Ypres. Little notice was taken of the Amiens sector or the steady decline in Second Army's fighting power. This lack of effective supervision of Marwitz' command suggests that Rupprecht must take some share of the blame for the surprise gained by the Allies at Amiens. (IWM Q 45520)

infiltration and surprise artillery bombardment tactics, particularly at the battle of Riga in September. In December 1917 he transferred to the Western Front to take command of Eighteenth Army in preparation for the coming offensives. His army formed the left flank during Operation *Michael*, and shattered the British Fifth Army south of the Somme. He was subsequently used to attack on the Matz in June where his tired troops were unable to reproduce their earlier success.

Generalleutnant Walter von Lüttwitz commanded III Corps on the right flank of the Eighteenth Army. Lüttwitz began the war as chief of staff of the Fourth Army before taking over command of 33rd Infantry Division in September 1914. In December 1915 he was promoted to command X Corps. From August to December 1916 he was chief of staff of Fifth Army defending against the French counteroffensive at Verdun. In November 1916 he took over command of III Corps which he led during Operation *Michael* under Hutier. **Generalleutnant Ritter und Edler Horst von Oetinger** commanded IX Corps. Oetinger commanded the 20th and 109th infantry divisions between 1914 and January 1917, seeing combat on the Marne, Galicia, Courland and Romania. In January 1917 he was promoted to command IX Corps which he led during Operation *Michael*. I Bavarian Corps was commanded by **Generalleutnant Ritter Nikolaus von Endres** and was formed during the battle on 10 August. Endres commanded an infantry brigade until March 1915, when he was promoted to command 4th Bavarian Infantry Division. He saw combat on the Somme (1914), Loos, Somme (1916) and at the battle of Third Ypres. In 1918 he fought at Kemmel before being promoted to command I Bavarian Corps in June.

The remaining corps of Eighteenth Army played only a peripheral role in the battle. I Reserve Corps was commanded by **Generalleutnant Kurt von Morgen**, XXVI Reserve Corps was commanded by **Generalleutnant Oskar von Watter** and XVIII Reserve Corps was commanded by **Generalleutnant Ludwig Sieger**.

OPPOSING ARMIES

BRITISH ARMY

The forces assembled for the battle of Amiens made Rawlinson's Fourth Army one of the strongest and most capable fielded by the BEF in the entire war. It contained some of the BEF's finest assault troops who were lavishly equipped with firepower and state-of-the-art technology. The presence of both Dominion corps gave Fourth Army a particular advantage. In addition to their larger size, which the Australians manned with volunteers only, both corps had a fixed divisional structure. This not only enhanced *esprit de corps* but also assisted training, strengthened command relationships and maximized performance in battle.

By 1918, British infantry platoons had new equipment and assault techniques. In addition to their rifles, the troops had been issued with Lewis guns, rifle grenades and hand grenades, which gave each platoon the ability to assault objectives independently by using direct and indirect fire to cover the attack of the riflemen and grenadiers. Such attacks were delivered using doctrine that placed a premium on assaulting from the flanks. There were usually four platoons to a company and four companies to a battalion.

The Lewis gun was introduced in 1914 and by 1918 was issued on a scale of two per platoon. It weighed 16kg when loaded and had could fire up to 100 rounds per minute. It had an effective range of 450m. (IWM E(Aus) 683)

RIGHT
An aerial photo showing a gun position at Chuignes. Together with flash spotting and sound ranging, Allied intelligence had located 504 of the 530 guns supporting Second Army. (IWM Q 55519)

BELOW RIGHT
A British 8in. howitzer is hauled into position prior to the offensive. Fourth Army had nine brigades of 8in. howitzers at Amiens, which it divided equally between its three corps. The 8in. howitzer fired a 90kg shell 9,600m. (IWM Q 2234)

Should the firepower of the infantry units prove insufficient, 3in., 6in. and 9.45in. mortar batteries were available at brigade, division and corps level respectively.

Notwithstanding the improvements to firepower based within infantry units, artillery remained the key to the techniques developed by the BEF in late 1917–18 for formal assaults. Better quality control of shell production and calibration of each gun enabled the batteries to fire much more accurately than previously. This was combined with more accurate maps and better target-acquisition technology, enabling the gunners to hit each target much more quickly without the need to range shots. Furthermore, rather than attempting to 'destroy' the German defences, the artillery now looked to 'neutralize' them just long enough for the infantry to mount the decisive assault. As a result the BEF dispensed with the prolonged bombardments that alerted the Germans to impending attacks between 1915 and late 1917, maximizing the chances of surprise. Each division had two field artillery brigades, each consisting of two batteries equipped with 18-pdr guns and one battery equipped with 4.5in. howitzers. Further field artillery brigades and heavy artillery batteries, equipped with 60-pdr and 6in. guns, and 6in., 8in., 9.2in. and 12in. howitzers were available at corps and army level.

The development of the Tank Corps had relieved the artillery of some of its infantry support tasks through the use of tanks to break through wire obstacles and directly assault German strongpoints where necessary. The improved Mk. V tank was the mainstay of the British tank force at Amiens. The Mk. V had a more powerful 150hp engine, an improved transmission and a better cooling system. It was armed with machine guns or 6-pdr cannon and had a top speed of 4.6mph. The Mk. Vs were complemented by the 'Whippet', which being less well protected and less heavily armed had a top speed of 8.3mph. A new model Mk. V, the Mk. V*, was introduced at Amiens. The Mk. V* was a basic Mk. V chassis that had been extended to include space for infantry machine-gun teams to be transported to deeper objectives. All the tanks, however, were uncomfortable for their crews, required heavy maintenance and lacked endurance on the battlefield.

Air support was provided by the newly formed Royal Air Force. Fourth Army was supported permanently by V Brigade RAF, which was reinforced by IX and III brigades RAF for the battle of Amiens. V Brigade consisted of a corps wing, an army wing and a balloon wing, whilst IX Brigade, as GHQ Reserve, consisted of two 'army' wings and a night operations wing. The corps wings assisted the balloon wing in controlling artillery fire close to the front line. The army wings were a mixed group of bomber, fighter and fighter-reconnaissance squadrons tasked with taking the aerial battle beyond the front line to protect the corps wing operating over German lines, as well as denying German observation aircraft the opportunity to operate over British lines.

A Mk V* tank in assault training with an infantry company prior to the battle. GHQ published a pamphlet (SS 204, *Training for an Infantry and Tank attack against Trenches*) in March 1918 directing the infantry to use the ground to advance in 'bounds' when operating with tanks. This can be clearly seen here as some sections lie in fire positions to cover others moving forward. The top right corner of the image is missing due to damage to the original plate. (IWM Q 9818)

Also attached to Fourth Army was the American 33rd Division, which was undergoing a period of training with the Australians to gain operational experience. The 33rd had been in France since May 1918 and, like all American divisions, at 28,000 men was substantially larger than its British and French counterparts. Each division was made up of two brigades, each containing two regiments of three infantry battalions and supporting units. Although the American doctrine emphasized open combat, little tactical detail was available to junior commanders. However, in the hardbitten Australian Corps, the 33rd Division had excellent tutors and their subsequent performance at Hamel demonstrated their training was not wasted.

Morale in the BEF was very good. Most of the Australian Corps and all of the Canadian Corps had been spared the trials of the defensive battles of the spring and early summer. They were well trained, well equipped, well rested and supremely confident in their leaders and themselves. Although lacking the élan of their Dominion colleagues, the British troops were dogged in defence and led by a cadre of junior leaders, significant numbers of whom had combat experience in offensive operations.

FRENCH ARMY

Although the French Army of 1918 was tactically effective in combat, four years of war had severely tempered the élan that characterized their earlier battles. Despite being tenacious in defence, unrest on the home front, high casualty rates and manpower shortages meant that morale was volatile. Mindful of this, Foch and his commanders envisaged limited attacks that maximized the use of firepower to spare their men.

The French Army had also developed the doctrine of firepower and surprise, augmented by tactical envelopment and flank attack for enemy strongpoints when necessary. Each division was usually made up of three regiments, each of three battalions. Although reduced in strength from 1,000 to 700 men, infantry battalions had been issued with 37mm cannon, 45mm

The 37mm cannon was issued to the French Infantry in 1916 with each battalion holding three in a trench artillery platoon. It weighed 108kg and had a maximum range of 2,400m. (IWM Q 953257)

and 60mm mortars, and had one rifle company converted to a machine-gun company to increase their firepower. The rifle platoons consisted of rifle, bombing and light machine-gun squads, and operated in a similar manner to their British counterparts. *Chasseur* battalions were created from the elite, prewar light infantry units attached to some divisions. They were larger than their line infantry counterparts, containing five instead of the normal three companies. The infantry formations contained significant numbers of units from the French colonies. The *zouaves* were recruited from Frenchmen living overseas and had gained a reputation as tough fighters. The *tirailleurs* were recruited from the indigenous populations of the colonies and had a more mixed reputation.

The artillery was the mainstay of French combat power, increasing from 20 per cent of the army in 1914 to 38 per cent by 1918. 105mm and 155mm guns and howitzers had augmented the prewar 75mm field guns. However, without the benefit of the heavier British tanks to assist with the tactical break-in, the French preferred to retain short, violent preparatory bombardments when organized defences were faced.

The most numerous French tank was the light Renault FT-17. At a weight of six tonnes and armed with a single machine gun or 37mm cannon, it lacked the firepower of the British tanks, but still operated as a mobile 'pillbox' in direct support of the infantry.

Unlike the British, the French air arm had not yet developed into a separate service. However, it had evolved similar structures to support the armies in battle. Each army controlled a number of fighter, reconnaissance and heavy artillery cooperation units giving it the ability to optimize and protect its own fire support, whilst at the same time disrupting that of the Germans. Each corps usually controlled a number of *escadrilles* to provide artillery liaison and close support to the divisional units. In early 1918 a large number of fighter and bomber *escadrilles* were grouped together into the Division Aérienne. This powerful formation was controlled by the French high command and deployed to the most important sector at a given time.

A section of Renault FT 17 tanks. Each section combined 37mm gun tanks (first left) with tanks equipped with Hotchkiss machine guns (second left). (IWM Q 58238)

GERMAN ARMY

The German Army at Amiens was a shadow of the force that had launched Operation *Michael* in March. Over 800,000 casualties had been sustained that could not be replaced. Worse still, the majority of these casualties had been sustained by elite assault units, which had been formed by stripping the youngest, fittest and most enterprising personnel from the line divisions. Furthermore the weakened army now had to defend a front extended from 390km to 510km in length.

Both the Second and Eighteenth armies had been at the forefront of Operation *Michael*. They received little respite in the ensuing months as reserves were continually withdrawn to support the offensives in Flanders and Champagne. The remaining divisions spent extended periods in the front line, and those in the Second Army suffered a constant attrition of strength to the aggressive Australian patrolling. This situation combined with poor food, and the apparent Allied resilience to attack fatally undermined the morale of the troops.

In these straitened circumstances, the Second and Eighteenth armies used a diluted variation of the defensive doctrine developed during the battles of 1916 and 1917. Foremost was a line of lightly held posts concealed in shell holes and other natural cover. These posts were to shield the main defensive line from Allied artillery observers and to disrupt any attacking force. The main defensive line was 1,500 to 2,000m farther back and held the majority of the front-line units. This line protected the artillery positions and was to be held at all costs. In each regimental sector the forward and main defensive positions were usually garrisoned with two battalions. The third battalion was held at rest 3,000 to 5,000m farther to the rear and acted as an immediate counterattack force. Behind the front-line divisions were the corps reserve divisions. Their role was to counterattack assaults that could not be dealt with by the front-line divisions on their own. Although this scheme originally saw

A German 'shell hole' post. Although relatively safe from artillery attack, and well supplied with hand grenades, these posts became increasingly vulnerable as the Australians developed their aggressive patrolling techniques. (IWM Q 23934)

one reserve behind each forward pair of divisions, the Second Army no longer had the manpower to maintain this ratio, with XI and LI corps both having one reserve division covering three and four in line respectively.

The core of the German Army was the infantry division, which consisted of three infantry regiments, each made up of three infantry battalions, an artillery command and supporting troops. Although each division had an establishment of 12,500 men, those of the Second Army were well under strength. By 1918 the main defensive weapon of the infantry was the machine gun. Each battalion had a machine-gun company with 12 guns, which were augmented by six light machine guns in each of the four rifle companies. The infantry battalions also had a mortar company with six 76mm mortars. These weapons would be sited to provide a deep, fire-swept zone through which attackers would need to advance.

In support of the infantry was the artillery command. This was made up by a field artillery regiment consisting of three battalions, each with three batteries equipped with 77mm field guns and 105mm light howitzers, and a heavy *Fuss* artillery battalion made up of two batteries of 150mm howitzers and one battery of 100mm guns. The divisional artillery was supported by batteries of heavier calibre guns under the control of corps and army HQs. The firepower they produced had the potential to shatter an Allied assault as it had many times before. However, under the new defence doctrine, lack of knowledge of German troop positions once counterattacks were under way made effective coordination with the infantry very difficult. Notwithstanding this weakness, German gun crews had demonstrated their effectiveness in engaging assaulting troops with direct fire after removing the guns from their gun pits. This tactic had been particularly successful against tanks that had lost the protection of supporting infantry at Cambrai in November 1917.

After Cambrai, Second Army also issued instructions on how tank attacks were to be fought. Tanks were to be allowed through the forward defensive positions, which would then hold up the supporting assault infantry. Once stripped of their infantry support, the tanks would then be destroyed by depth positions using machine guns, anti-tank rifles, trench mortars and bundled hand grenades.

The Luftstreitkräfte remained a powerful adversary in the summer of 1918. Equipped with excellent aircraft and manned by a cadre of high quality and experienced aircrew, the *Schlachtstaffeln* (Schlastas) and *Jagdstaffeln* (Jastas) were concentrated on areas of the front where the need was greatest with a smaller proportion permanently assigned to specific sectors. The Schlastas were equipped mainly with the two-seater Hannover CLII and III, and Halberstadt CLII and IV aircraft, and specialized in low-level attacks on enemy troops with both machine guns and light bombs. Since May 1918, many of the Jastas had been re-equipped with the new Fokker DVII, which utilized new engine and aerodynamic technologies to outperform its rivals. The Jastas could be formed into temporary *Jagdgruppen* in a specific sector when necessary, whilst 12 Jastas had been permanently grouped into three *Jagdgeschwader* (JG I, JG II, JG III) between June 1917 and February 1918.

Reconnaissance and artillery cooperation was effected via the *Fliegerabteilung* (FA) and *Fliegerabteilung (Artillerie)* (FA (A)) units.

During major combat operations the Jastas were normally controlled at army level to ensure concentration of force, whilst control of the FAs, FA(A)s and Schlastas was usually devolved to corps level to ensure better integration with the ground battle.

ORDERS OF BATTLE

BRITISH ARMY, 8 AUGUST 1918

FOURTH ARMY – GEN. SIR HENRY RAWLINSON

III Corps – Lt. Gen. Sir R. H. K. Butler
47th Division – Maj. Gen. Sir G. F. Gorringe
140th Brigade
15th London
17th London
21st London
141st Brigade
18th London
19th London
20th London
142nd Brigade
22nd London
23rd London
24th London
12th Division – Maj. Gen. H. W. Higginson
35th Brigade
7th Norfolk
9th Essex
1/1st Cambridgeshire
36th Brigade
9th Royal Fusiliers
7th Royal Sussex
5th Royal Berkshire
37th Brigade
6th Queens (Royal West Surrey)
6th Buffs (East Kent)
6th Royal West Kent
18th Division – Maj. Gen. R. P. Lee
53rd Brigade
10th Essex
8th Royal Berkshire
7th Royal West Kent
54th Brigade
11th Royal Fusiliers
2nd Bedfordshire
6th Northamptonshire
55th Brigade
7th Queens (Royal West Surrey)
7th Buffs (East Kent)
8th East Surrey
58th Division – Maj. Gen. F. W. Ramsey
173rd Brigade
2/2nd London
3rd London
2/4th London
174th Brigade
6th London
7th London
8th London
175th Brigade
9th London
2/10th London
12th London
10th Tank Battalion – 36 Mk V tanks

Australian Corps – Lt. Gen. Sir J. Monash
1st Australian Division – Maj. Gen. T. W. Glasgow
1st Australian Brigade
1st (New South Wales) Bn.
2nd (New South Wales) Bn.
3rd (New South Wales) Bn.
4th (New South Wales) Bn.
2nd Australian Brigade
5th (Victoria) Bn.
6th (Victoria) Bn.
7th (Victoria) Bn.
8th (Victoria) Bn.
3rd Australian Brigade
9th (Queensland) Bn.
10th (South Australia) Bn.
11th (Western Australia) Bn.
12th (Tasmania) Bn.
2nd Australian Division – Maj. Gen. C. Rosenthal
5th Australian Brigade
17th (New South Wales) Bn.

18th (New South Wales) Bn.
19th (New South Wales) Bn.
20th (New South Wales) Bn.
6th Australian Brigade
21st (Victoria) Bn.
22nd (Victoria) Bn.
23rd (Victoria) Bn.
24th (Victoria) Bn.
7th Australian Brigade
25th (Queensland) Bn.
26th (Queensland) Bn.
27th (South Australia) Bn.
28th (Western Australia) Bn.
3rd Australian Division – Maj. Gen. J. Gellibrand
9th Australian Brigade
33rd (New South Wales) Bn.
34th (New South Wales) Bn.
35th (New South Wales) Bn.
36th (New South Wales) Bn.
10th Australian Brigade
37th (Victoria) Bn.
38th (Victoria) Bn.
39th (Victoria) Bn.
40th (Tasmania) Bn.
11th Australian Brigade
41st (Queensland) Bn.
42nd (Queensland) Bn.
43rd (South Australia) Bn.
44th (Western Australia) Bn.
4th Australian Division – Maj. Gen. E. Sinclair-Maclagan
4th Australian Brigade
13th (New South Wales) Bn.
14th (Victoria) Bn.
15th (Queensland and Tasmania) Bn.
16th (Western Australia and South Australia) Bn.
12th Australian Brigade
45th (New South Wales) Bn.
46th (Victoria) Bn.
48th (South Australia and Western Australia) Bn.
13th Australian Brigade
49th (Queensland) Bn.
50th (South Australia) Bn.
51st (Western Australia) Bn.
5th Australian Division – Maj. Gen. J. J. Talbot-Hobbs
8th Australian Brigade
29th (Victoria) Bn.
30th (New South Wales) Bn.
31st (Queensland and Victoria) Bn.
32nd (South Australia and West Australia) Bn.
14th Australian Brigade
53rd (New South Wales) Bn.
54th (New South Wales) Bn.
55th (New South Wales) Bn.
56th (New South Wales) Bn.
15th Australian Brigade
57th (Victoria) Bn.
58th (Victoria) Bn.
59th (Victoria) Bn.
60th (Victoria) Bn.
5th Tank Brigade
2nd Tank Battalion – 36 Mk. V tanks
8th Tank Battalion – 36 Mk. V tanks
13th Tank Battalion – 36 Mk. V tanks
15th Tank Battalion – 36 Mk. V* tanks
17th Armoured Car Battalion – 16 cars

Canadian Corps – Lt. Gen. Sir A. Currie
1st Canadian Division – Maj. Gen. A. C. Macdonell
1st Canadian Brigade
1st (Western Ontario) Bn.
2nd (Eastern Ontario) Bn.
3rd (Toronto) Bn.
4th (Central Ontario) Bn.
2nd Canadian Brigade
5th (Western Cavalry) Bn.
7th (1st British Columbia) Bn.
8th (90th Rifles) Bn.
10th (Canadians) Bn.

3rd Canadian Brigade
13th (Royal Highlanders of Canada) Bn.
14th (Royal Montreal) Bn.
15th (48th Highlanders of Canada) Bn.
16th (The Canadian Scottish) Bn.
2nd Canadian Division – Maj. Gen. Sir H. E. Burstall
4th Canadian Brigade
18th (Western Ontario) Bn.
19th (Western Ontario) Bn.
20th (Central Ontario) Bn.
21st (Eastern Ontario) Bn.
5th Canadian Brigade
22nd (French Canadian) Bn.
24th (Victoria Rifles of Canada) Bn.
25th (Nova Scotia Rifles) Bn.
26th (New Brunswick) Bn.
6th Canadian Brigade
27th (City of Winnipeg) Bn.
28th (North West) Bn.
29th (Vancouver) Bn.
31st (Alberta) Bn.
3rd Canadian Division – Maj. Gen. L. J. Lipsett
7th Canadian Brigade
Princess Patricia's Canadian Light Infantry
The Royal Canadian Regiment
42nd (Royal Highlanders of Canada) Bn.
49th (Edmonton) Bn.
8th Canadian Brigade
1st Canadian Mounted Rifles*
2nd Canadian Mounted Rifles*
4th Canadian Mounted Rifles*
5th Canadian Mounted Rifles*
9th Canadian Brigade
43rd (Cameron Highlanders of Canada) Bn.
52nd (New Ontario) Bn.
58th (Central Ontario) Bn.
116th (Ontario County) Bn.
4th Canadian Division – Maj. Gen. Sir D. Watson
10th Canadian Brigade
44th (New Brunswick) Bn.
46th (South Saskatchewan) Bn.
47th (Western Ontario) Bn.
50th (Calgary) Bn.
11th Canadian Brigade
54th (Central Ontario) Bn.
75th (Mississauga) Bn.
87th (Canadian Grenadier Guards) Bn.
102nd (Central Ontario) Bn.
12th Canadian Brigade
38th (Ottawa) Bn.
72nd (Seaforth Highlanders of Canada) Bn.
78th (Winnipeg Grenadiers) Bn.
85th (Nova Scotia Highlanders) Bn.
4th Tank Brigade
1st Tank Battalion – 36 Mk.V* tanks
4th Tank Battalion – 36 Mk. V tanks
5th Tank Battalion – 36 Mk. V tanks
14th Tank Battalion – 36 Mk. V tanks

Cavalry Corps – Lt. Gen. Sir C. Kavanagh
1st Cavalry Division – Maj. Gen. R. L. Mullens
1st Cavalry Brigade
2nd Dragoon Guards (The Queen's Bays)
5th Dragoon Guards
11th Hussars
2nd Cavalry Brigade
4th Dragoon Guards
9th Royal Lancers
18th Hussars
9th Cavalry Brigade
8th Hussars
15th Hussars
19th Hussars
2nd Cavalry Division – Maj. Gen. T. T. Pitman
3rd Cavalry Brigade
4th Hussars
5th Royal Lancers
16th Lancers

4th Cavalry Brigade
 6th Dragoon Guards (Carabineers)
 3rd Hussars
 1st (Queen's Own Oxfordshire) Hussars
5th Cavalry Brigade
 2nd Dragoons (Royal Scots Greys)
 12th Royal Lancers
 20th Hussars
3rd Cavalry Division – Maj. Gen. A. E. W. Harman
6th Cavalry Brigade
 3rd Dragoon Guards
 1st (Royal) Dragoons
 10th Hussars
7th Cavalry Brigade
 7th Dragoon Guards
 6th (Inniskilling) Dragoons
 17th Lancers
Can Cavalry Brigade
 Royal Canadian Dragoons
 Lord Strathcona's Horse
 Fort Garry Horse
3rd Tank Brigade
 3rd Tank Battalion – 36 'Whippet' tanks
 6th Tank Battalion – 36 'Whippet' tanks

GHQ Reserve
17th Division – Maj. Gen. P. R. Robertson
50th Brigade
 10th West Yorkshire
 7th East Yorkshire
 6th Dorsetshire
51st Brigade
 7th Lincolns
 7th Border
 10th Sherwood Foresters
52nd Brigade
 10th Lancashire Fusiliers
 9th Duke of Wellington's
 12th Manchester
32nd Division – Maj. Gen. T. S. Lambert
14th Brigade
 5th/6th Royal Scots
 1st Dorsetshire
 15th Highland Light Infantry
96th Brigade
 15th Lancashire Fusiliers
 16th Lancashire Fusiliers
 2nd Manchester
97th Brigade
 1/5th Border
 2nd King's Own Yorkshire Light Infantry
 10th Argyll and Sutherland Highlanders
63rd (RN) Division – Maj. Gen. C. E. Lawrie
188th Brigade
 Anson Bn.
 1st Royal Marines
 2nd Royal Irish
189th Brigade
 Hood Bn.
 Hawke Bn.
 Drake Bn.
190th Brigade
 1/4th Bedfordshire
 1/28th London
 7th Royal Fusiliers
9th Tank Battalion – 36 Mk V tanks

Training with Fourth Army
33rd (US) Division – Maj. Gen. G. Bell Jnr
65th Brigade
 129th Infantry Regiment
 130th Infantry Regiment
66th Brigade
 131st Infantry Regiment
 132nd Infantry Regiment

Royal Air Force – Maj. Gen. J. M. Salmond
V Brigade
 15th (Corps) Wing – 110 aircraft
  Six corps squadrons
 22nd (Army) Wing – 222 aircraft

  Eight fighter squadrons
  One fighter-recce squadron
  One day-bomber squadron
  One night-bomber squadron
IX Brigade
 9th Wing – 99 aircraft
  Two fighter squadrons
  Two bomber squadrons
  One fighter-recce squadron
 51st Wing – 101 aircraft
  Three fighter squadrons
  Two bomber squadrons
 54th Wing – 76 aircraft
  Two night-fighter squadron
  Four night-bomber squadrons
III Brigade (available in support)
 13th (Army) Wing – 136 aircraft
  Four fighter squadrons
  One day-bomber squadron
  One night-bomber squadron
  One fighter-recce squadron
I Brigade (available in support) – 19 aircraft
 One day-bomber squadron
X Brigade (available in support) – 19 aircraft
 One day-bomber squadron

Corps aircraft	110
Fighters	376
Fighter-recce	75
Day-bombers	147
Night-bombers	92
Total air strength	800

All organized as dismounted infantry battalions

FRENCH ARMY, 8 AUGUST 1918

FIRST ARMY – GÉN. EUGENE DEBENEY

XXXI Corps – Gén. Toulorge
37th Division
 2nd Zouave Regiment
 3rd Zouave Regiment
 2nd Tirailleur Regiment
42nd Division
 94th Infantry Regiment
 332nd Infantry Regiment
 8th Battalion de Chasseurs à Pied
 16th Battalion de Chasseurs à Pied
66th Division
 7th Groupe de Chasseurs Alpins
 8th Groupe de Chasseurs Alpins
 9th Groupe de Chasseurs Alpins
153rd Division
 9th Zouave Regiment
 1st Moroccan Tirailleur Regiment
 418th Infantry Regiment
 9th Battalion de Chars Légers
 11th Battalion de Chars Légers
126th Division
 55th Infantry Regiment
 112th Infantry Regiment
 173rd Infantry Regiment
Six escadrilles – 60 aircraft

IX Corps – Gén. Garnier du Plessis
3rd Division
 51st Infantry Regiment
 87th Infantry Regiment
 272nd Infantry Regiment
15th Colonial Division
 2nd Colonial Infantry Regiment
 5th Colonial Infantry Regiment
 6th Colonial Infantry Regiment
Four escadrilles – 40 aircraft

X Corps – Gén. Vandenburg
60th Division
 202nd Infantry Regiment

 225th Infantry Regiment
 248th Infantry Regiment
152nd Division
 114th Infantry Regiment
 125th Infantry Regiment
 135th Infantry Regiment
166th Division
 171st Infantry Regiment
 294th Infantry Regiment
 19th Battalion de Chasseurs à Pied
 26th Battalion de Chasseurs à Pied
Three escadrilles – 30 aircraft

XXXV Corps – Gén. Jaquot
46th Division
 1st Groupe de Chasseurs à Pied
 2nd Groupe de Chasseurs à Pied
 3rd Groupe de Chasseurs à Pied
133rd Division
 321st Infantry Regiment
 401st Infantry Regiment
 15th Groupe de Chasseurs à Pied
169th Division
 13th Infantry Regiment
 29th Infantry Regiment
 39th Infantry Regiment
Five escadrilles – 50 aircraft

II Cavalry Corps – Gén. Robillot
2nd Cavalry Division
 2nd Light Cavalry Brigade
 2nd Dragoon Brigade
 12th Dragoon Brigade
4th Cavalry Division
 4th Light Cavalry Brigade
 4th Dragoon Brigade
 3rd Cuirassier Brigade
6th Cavalry Division
 6th Light Cavalry Brigade
 6th Dragoon Brigade

Army support air units
Groupe de Chasse 12 – 90 aircraft
Groupe de Chasse 16 – 90 aircraft
Three reconnaissance escadrilles – 30 aircraft
Three artillery support escadrilles – 35 aircraft
One night-bomber escadre – 52 aircraft

THIRD ARMY – GÉN. HUMBERT

XV Corps – Gén. de Fonclare
67th Division
 283rd Infantry Regiment
 288th Infantry Regiment
 369th Infantry Regiment
74th Division
 230th Infantry Regiment
 299th Infantry Regiment
 16th Groupe de Chasseurs a Pied
123rd Division
 6th Infantry Regiment
 12th Infantry Regiment
 411th Infantry Regiment

XXXIV Corps – Gén. Nudant
6th Division
 24th Infantry Regiment
 28th Infantry Regiment
 119th Infantry Regiment
121st Division
 36th Infantry Regiment
 404th Infantry Regiment
 11th Groupe de Chasseurs à Pied
129th Division
 297th Infantry Regiment
 14th Tirailleur Regiment
 12th Groupe de Chasseurs à Pied
165th Division
 154th Infantry Regiment
 155th Infantry Regiment
 287th Infantry Regiment

Army reserve
1st Division
  1st Infantry Regiment
  201st Infantry Regiment
  233rd Infantry Regiment

La Division Aérienne
I Brigade
  Escadre 1 – 190 aircraft
    Groupe de Chasse 15
    Groupe de Chasse 18
    Groupe de Chasse 19
  Escadre 12 – 135 aircraft
    Groupe de Bombardement 5
    Groupe de Bombardement 6
    Groupe de Bombardement 9
II Brigade
  Escadre 2 – 195 aircraft
    Groupe de Chasse 13
    Groupe de Chasse 17
    Groupe de Chasse 20
  Escadre 13 – 90 aircraft
    Groupe de Bombardement 3
    Groupe de Bombardement 4
  Groupe Laurens – 52 aircraft
    Groupe de Bombardement (nuit) 8
    Groupe de Bombardement (nuit) 10
  Groupe Weiller
    Escadrille 220
    Bréguet 45
    Spad 313

Corps aircraft	180
Army aircraft:	
Fighters	180
Night-bombers	52
Corps support	65
Division Aerienne:	
Fighters	432
Bombers	195
Total air strength	1,104

GERMAN ARMY, 8 AUGUST 1918

SECOND ARMY – GEN. VON DER MARWITZ

LIV Corps – Gen.Lt. von Larisch
27th Division
  120th Infantry Regiment
  123rd Infantry Regiment
  124th Infantry Regiment
54th Reserve Division – Gen.Maj. Kabisch
  246th Reserve Infantry Regiment
  247th Reserve Infantry Regiment
  248th Reserve Infantry Regiment
233rd Division
  448th Infantry Regiment
  449th Infantry Regiment
  450th Infantry Regiment
243rd Division
  122nd Infantry Regiment
  478th Reserve Infantry Regiment
  479th Infantry Regiment
26th Reserve Division – from Seventeenth Army,
9 August
  180th Infantry Regiment
  119 Reserve Infantry Regiment
  121 Reserve Infantry Regiment

XI Corps – Gen.Lt. Kühne
13th Division
  13th Infantry Regiment
  15th Infantry Regiment
  55th Infantry Regiment
41st Division
  18th Infantry Regiment
  148th Infantry Regiment
  152nd Infantry Regiment

43rd Reserve Division
  201st Reserve Infantry Regiment
  202nd Reserve Infantry Regiment
  203rd Reserve Infantry Regiment
108th Division
  97th Infantry Regiment
  137th Infantry Regiment
  265th Reserve Infantry Regiment
107th Division – from Second Army reserve, 8 August
  52nd Reserve Infantry Regiment
  232nd Reserve Infantry Regiment
  448th Infantry Regiment
21st Division– from Second Army reserve, 9 August
  80th Infantry Regiment
  81st Infantry Regiment
  87th Infantry Regiment
5th Bavarian Division – from Seventeenth Army,
8 August
  7th Bavarian Infantry Regiment
  19th Bavarian Infantry Regiment
  21st Bavarian Infantry Regiment
38th Division – from Sixth Army, 9 August
  94th Infantry Regiment
  95th Infantry Regiment
  96th Infantry Regiment

LI Corps – Gen.Lt. von Hofacker
14th Bavarian Division
  4th Bavarian Infantry Regiment
  8th Bavarian Infantry Regiment
  25th Bavarian Infantry Regiment
109th Division
  2nd Grenadier Infantry Regiment
  26th Reserve Infantry Regiment
  376th Infantry Regiment
117th Division – Gen.Maj. Höfer
  11th Infantry Regiment
  157th Infantry Regiment
  450th Infantry Regiment
192nd Division
  183rd Infantry Regiment
  192nd Infantry Regiment
  245th Reserve Infantry Regiment
225th Division – Gen.Lt. von Woyna
  373rd Infantry Regiment
  18th Reserve Infantry Regiment
  217th Reserve Infantry Regiment

Luftstreitkräfte
Jagdgruppe 2
Jagdgruppe Greim
Bombengeschwader 7
Fliegerabteilung (Lichtbildgerät) 40
Fliegerabteilung 17, 33
Fliegerabteilung (Artillerie) 217,224,207, 219, 232,
241, 269
Schlachtstaffeln 17

EIGHTEENTH ARMY – GEN. VON HUTIER

III Corps – Gen.Lt. von Lüttwitz
24th Division
  133rd Infantry Regiment
  139th Infantry Regiment
  179th Infantry Regiment
25th Reserve Division
  168th Infantry Regiment
  83rd Reserve Infantry Regiment
  118th Reserve Infantry Regiment
1st Reserve Division
  1st Reserve Infantry Regiment
  3rd Reserve Infantry Regiment
  59th Reserve Infantry Regiment
79th Reserve Division – from Seventh Army, 9 August
  261st Reserve Infantry Regiment
  262nd Reserve Infantry Regiment
  263rd Reserve Infantry Regiment

IX Corps – Gen.Lt. von Oetinger
2nd Division – Gen.Maj. von Dommes

  4th Grenadier Infantry Regiment
  33rd Fusilier Infantry Regiment
  44th Infantry Regiment
11th Division
  10th Grenadier Infantry Regiment
  38th Fusilier Infantry Regiment
  51st Infantry Regiment
82nd Reserve Division – two regiments to III Corps,
8 August
  270th Reserve Infantry Regiment
  271st Reserve Infantry Regiment
  272nd Reserve Infantry Regiment

I Reserve Corps – Gen.Lt. von Morgen
75th Reserve Division
  249th Reserve Infantry Regiment
  250th Reserve Infantry Regiment
  251st Reserve Infantry Regiment
206th Division
  359th Infantry Regiment
  394th Infantry Regiment
  4th Reserve Ersatz Infantry Regiment
119th Division – to LI Corps, Second Army, 8 August
  46th Infantry Regiment
  46th Reserve Infantry Regiment
  58th Infantry Regiment

XXVI Corps – Gen.Lt. von Watter
17th Reserve Division
  162nd Infantry Regiment
  163rd Infantry Regiment
  76th Reserve Infantry Regiment
54th Division
  84th Infantry Regiment
  27th Reserve Infantry Regiment
  90th Reserve Infantry Regiment
204th Division – to I Bavarian Corps, 10 August
  413th Infantry Regiment
  414th Infantry Regiment
  120th Reserve Infantry Regiment

XVIII Reserve Corps – Gen.Lt. Sieger
3rd Bavarian Division
  17th Bavarian Infantry Regiment
  18th Bavarian Infantry Regiment
  23rd Bavarian Infantry Regiment
105th Division – Gen.Lt. Ehrhardt
  21st Infantry Regiment
  129th Infantry Regiment
  400th Infantry Regiment
221st Division – Gen.Lt. von La Chevallerie – to III Corps,
9 August
  41st Infantry Regiment
  60th Reserve Infantry Regiment
  45th Infantry Regiment

**I Bavarian Corps – Gen.Lt. Ritter von Endres
(formed 10 August)**
Alpenkorps – from Fourth Army, 10 August
  Lieb Infantry Regiment
  1st Bavarian Jäger Regiment
  2nd Jäger Regiment
121st Division – Gen.Maj. Bressler – from Ninth Army,
10 August
  60th Infantry Regiment
  7th Reserve Infantry Regiment
  56th Reserve Infantry Regiment

Luftstreitkräfte
Jagdstaffeln 24, 42, 44, 78
Bombengeschwader 4
Fliegerabteilung (Lichtbildgerät) 23
Fliegerabteilung (Artillerie) 2, 245, 14, 212, 238, 203
Schlachtstaffeln 36

Corps aircraft	171
Fighters	140
Bombers	36
Battle fighters	18
Total Strength	365 aircraft

OPPOSING PLANS

ALLIED PLANS

The plan that Rawlinson developed marked the zenith of operational and tactical performance within the BEF during World War I. The key contribution from his perspective was the maintenance of surprise, which he achieved by the covert assembly of the assault force. Knowing the significance placed by the Germans on the elite Canadian Corps, Haig and Rawlinson not only shielded their movement from Arras to Amiens, but devised a sophisticated deception plan using false radio traffic and limited movement of troops to imitate a move to the Ypres sector in the north. Once safely hidden in the Amiens area, the Canadians were also held back from the front line until two hours before the attack was launched. Tank and artillery positions were camouflaged and dissemination of the plan was strictly controlled.

Rawlinson's initial plan proposed the old Amiens 'Outer Defence Line' as the objective with the option that the Cavalry Corps could continue the advance to the south east should the opportunity arise. Both Haig and Foch were concerned that this was too cautious. Consequently, on 26 July Rawlinson and Debeney were directed to strike for the deeper objectives of Chaulnes and Roye.

To assist surprise, artillery ammunition was pre-dumped and camouflaged at battery positions. The position would be occupied by the guns only at the last moment in order to avoid detection by German reconnaissance aircraft. (IWM E(Aus) 3888)

The development of the tactical plans for the battle demonstrated the high level of proficiency and flexibility of the BEF by the summer of 1918. The three corps of the Fourth Army were to reach the Amiens Outer Defence Line in three stages. The advance to the first objective (Green Line) was to be achieved under a creeping barrage. The advance to the second objective (Black Line) was to be covered by mobile artillery batteries moving forwards and tanks. The advance to the third objective (Red Line) was to be achieved initially by the Cavalry Corps, supported by Whippet tanks and Mk V* tanks each carrying infantry machine-gun crews who were to dismount on arrival at the objective. These would be followed up by the final elements of the attacking infantry

The size of the armoured force to be committed was greatly increased in the planning phase. After advice from Tank Corps HQ, Rawlinson agreed to use the entire Tank Corps in the attack, deploying 342 Mk V and Mk V*, 72 Whippet and 120 supply tanks. The 4th and 5th tank brigades were allotted to the Canadian and Australian corps respectively, whilst III Corps received one battalion and the Cavalry Corps the two battalions of Whippets.

Despite the similarity of their tasks, Monash and Currie produced different schemes of manoeuvre for their respective corps. Monash chose to maintain a level of personal control over the battle by 'leapfrogging' his divisions as the attack progressed. The 2nd and 3rd Australian divisions were to seize the first objective, at which point the 4th and 5th Australian divisions would pass through them to seize the second and third objectives. Currie took a slightly different approach by delegating control to the commanders of 1st and 2nd Canadian divisions, who were to 'leapfrog' their brigades to the third objective. Only in the south of the Canadian Corps sector would the 3rd Canadian Division stop short, being 'leapfrogged' by the 4th Canadian Division at the second objective to complete the attack. North of the Somme, Butler's III Corps would attack with the 12th, 18th and 58th divisions in line to form a defensive flank to the left of the Australian Corps.

The 3rd Cavalry Division and the 1st Cavalry Brigade were attached to the Canadian and Australian corps respectively, to assist with the securing of

An oblique aerial view from above Villers-Bretonneux. The boundary between the Australian and Canadian sectors ran along the railway running from the bottom right of the photograph. (IWM Q 52079)

the third objective. The 1st and 2nd cavalry divisions were to follow up the Canadian attack and drive on Chaulnes and Roye if the opportunity presented itself.

The Fourth Army benefited from a sophisticated plan for air support from the RAF. Prior to the battle, secrecy was to be assisted by preventing German reconnaissance aircraft from penetrating Allied airspace during the concentration of the assault troops. At the opening of the battle, air superiority was to be achieved by a dawn strike on the German airfields by the bombers of V and IX brigades, with the fighters of IX and III brigades providing the subsequent air cover against any intruding German aircraft. Once the assault began, the fighters of 22nd (Army) Wing were tasked to fly close air support missions, each armed with 25lb bombs and machine guns. Meanwhile, the corps support aircraft were to conduct the innovative tasks of parachute re-supply of ammunition to forward troops and the dropping of smoke bombs to screen movement in addition to their traditional roles. The bombers were scheduled to return to the fray with evening strikes against the Péronne and Chaulnes railway stations in an attempt to hinder the anticipated arrival of reinforcements to the area.

Debeney's task was made more difficult by terrain and his lack of armoured forces in comparison with the British. The front line turned from south-west to south-east having crossed the Avre at Moreuil. In order to assist the difficult assault river crossings, Debeney placed his main effort with XXXI Corps, between the Canadian Corps and the Avre, in order to threaten the German defences on the Avre from the rear. Once this was achieved, the second phase of the attack would see the right of XXXI Corps and IX Corps assaulting across the river. The 42nd and 37th divisions would spearhead the attack of XXXI Corps with the 153rd Division providing the second echelon. The 66th Division would capture Moreuil by envelopment, whilst farther south in the IX Corps the 15th Colonial and 3rd divisions were to cross the Avre at Braches.

Owing to the absence of heavy armour to support the attack, Debeney chose to delay his infantry assault until a short but intense artillery

The wreckage of supply tanks whose cargo was ignited by German artillery fire at Villers-Bretonneux on 7 August. The supply tanks were originally designed as gun-carrying vehicles and 48 were built and deployed in 1917. Although they were capable of carrying 60-pdr or 6in. howitzer weapons, their self-propelled artillery capability was discontinued and they were 'relegated' to supply duties. Each vehicle could carry the equivalent of the supply load of 300 men. (IWM E(Aus) 3908)

bombardment was completed. The bombardment was to open at the same time as the British attack in the north in order to maintain surprise, with the infantry assaulting 45 minutes later. Two battalions of light tanks were to deploy in support of the 153rd Division as it entered the line.

The X, XXXV and II Cavalry corps were to enter the attack on the second day. X Corps was to cross the Avre at Pierrepont and cover the continuing advance of XXXI Corps to the north. Meanwhile, XXXV Corps was to attack south of Montdidier at Assainvillers and open the way for the II Cavalry Corps to advance on Roye.

Humbert's Third Army was to join the attack on 10 August, with the XXXIV and XV corps covering the right flank of the First Army.

GERMAN PLANS

So effective were the security measures imposed by the British and French, Marwitz and Hutier had little inkling of the assault that was about to hit them and consequently had few detailed plans beyond the generic German defensive scheme. Complacency permeated the German command structure from top to bottom with little notice being taken of the increasing difficulty in penetrating the Allied airspace suffered by their reconnaissance aircraft. Defensive positions, although marked on staff planning maps, were in reality just marked out in tape on the ground with little sense of urgency to complete them. Even an inspection by Kuhl, Rupprecht's chief of staff, raised little concern short of allocating the fresh 117th Division to the sector.

In the Second Army the LIV, XI and LI corps had ten divisions in line and four divisions in reserve. One of the front-line divisions, the 27th, mounted an attack on the British 58th and 18th divisions south of Morlancourt on 6 August. The attack drove the British back 750m on a 4km front and captured 236 prisoners. However, despite the disruption caused to the plans, the prisoners divulged nothing to their captors who remained ignorant of the impending assault. Indeed, such was the level of surprise achieved by the Allies, XI Corps was in the process of relieving the 43rd Division with the 108th Division from reserve on the night of 7/8 August.

THE BATTLE OF AMIENS

8 AUGUST 1918

The night of 7/8 August was generally quiet and as the Allies began to move the assault troops into position, a thick mist rose from the river valleys shrouding the surrounding countryside. At 0420hrs on 8 August, the 3,700 guns of the British and French artillery crashed out the first salvoes of the opening bombardment and Fourth Army commenced its assault.

The first phase – breaking the line

North of the Somme, the first phase of III Corps' attack was delivered by the 18th and 58th divisions and, owing to the combined effects of the German attack on 6 August, the thick mist and the fact that the attack hit the boundary of the German LIV and XI Corps, it was a confused engagement for both sides.

The 58th Division attacked with the 6th and 7th Londons of the 174th Brigade and the 2/10th Londons of the 175th Brigade, with C Company of the 10th Tank Battalion in support. The objective of the 174th Brigade was

An oblique aerial view of the 58th Division sector. The British front line runs through the two dark fields just beyond the lane in the bottom right foreground. The German front line runs through the dark field running parallel to the lane. The first objective was on the far edge of Malard Wood. The southern tip of Gressaire Wood is in the top left corner and the Chipilly Spur runs across the centre. According to German records, the 265th Reserve Infantry Regiment 'was liquidated' by the 174th Brigade in this area. (IWM Q 61681)

8 August 1918, 'The Black Day'.

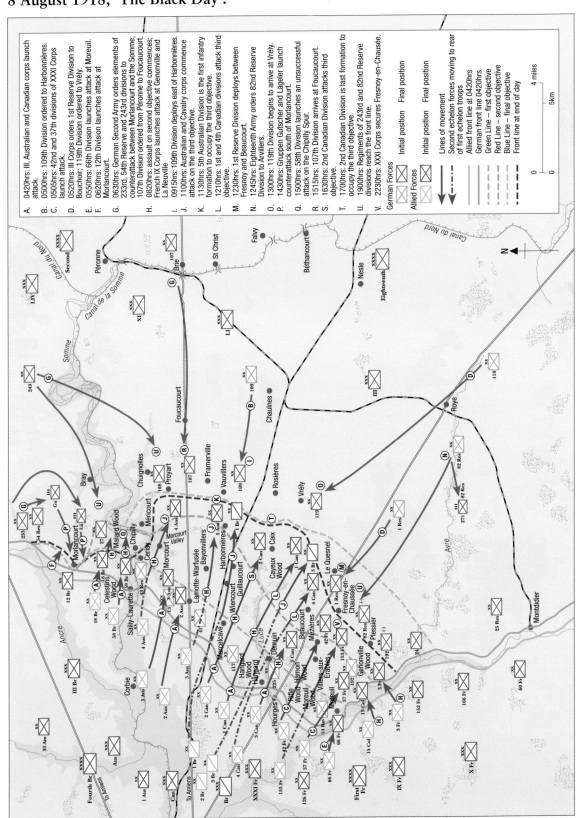

A. 0420hrs: III, Australian and Canadian corps launch attack.
B. 0500hrs: 109th Division ordered to Harbonnières.
C. 0505hrs: 42nd and 37th divisions of XXXI Corps launch attack.
D. 0520hrs: III Corps orders 1st Reserve Division to Bouchoir; 119th Division ordered to Vrély.
E. 0550hrs: 66th Division launches attack at Moreuil.
F. 0620hrs: 12th Division launches attack at Morlancourt.
G. 0630hrs: German Second Army orders elements of 233rd, 54th Reserve and 243rd divisions to counterattack between Morlancourt and the Somme; 107th Division ordered from Péronne to Foucaucourt.
H. 0820hrs: assault on second objective commences; French IX Corps launches attack at Genonville and La Neuville.
I. 0915hrs: 109th Division deploys east of Harbonnières.
J. 1100hrs: Australian and Cavalry corps commence attack on the third objective.
K. 1130hrs: 5th Australian Division is the first infantry formation to occupy the third objective.
L. 1210hrs: 1st and 4th Canadian divisions attack third objective.
M. 1230hrs: 1st Reserve Division deploys between Fresnoy and Beaucourt.
N. 1245hrs: Eighteenth Army orders 82nd Reserve Division to Arvillers.
O. 1300hrs: 119th Division begins to arrive at Vrély.
P. 1430hrs: Gruppen Gutscher and Lägeler launch counterattack south of Morlancourt.
Q. 1500hrs: 58th Division launches an unsuccessful attack on the Chipilly Spur.
R. 1515hrs: 107th Division arrives at Foucaucourt.
S. 1630hrs: 2nd Canadian Division attacks third objective.
T. 1700hrs: 2nd Canadian Division is last formation to occupy the third objective.
U. 1900hrs: Regiments of 243rd and 82nd Reserve divisions reach the front line.
V. 2230hrs: XXXI Corps secures Fresnoy-en-Chaussée.

German Forces
Allied Forces

Initial position   Final position
Initial position   Final position

Lines of movement
Second echelon forces moving to rear of first echelon troops
Allied front line at 0420hrs
German front line 0420hrs
Green Line – first objective
Red Line – second objective
Blue Line – final objective
Front line at end of day

0   4 miles
0   5km

Sailly-Laurette after its capture by the 2/10th Londons, showing the devastation wrought by the artillery barrage. III Corps was supported by 17 field artillery brigades, eight heavy artillery brigades, three 6in. gun batteries and one 12in. howitzer batteries for the assault at Amiens. (IWM Q 6912)

Malard Wood, whilst the 2/10th Londons cleared Sailly-Laurette. Despite the mist preventing the tanks from following the infantry closely, the Londons quickly infiltrated and overran the forward positions of the 265th Reserve Infantry Regiment, and by 0800hrs the first objective on the eastern side of Malard Wood had been reached.

The assault of the 2/10th Londons caught the 201st Reserve Infantry Regiment of the 43rd Reserve Division as the 137th Infantry Regiment of the 108th Division was relieving it. The Londons secured Sailly-Laurette by 0700hrs, and then pushed on towards Chipilly.

Farther north, the 18th Division had been forced to relieve the 54th Brigade with the 36th Brigade of the 12th Division due to the losses incurred during the German attack on 6 August. Unfamiliar with the ground over which they would need to fight, the 36th Brigade attacked together with the 55th Brigade. Instead of waiting to meet the assault from defensive positions, some of the Württemburgers of the 120th and 123rd infantry regiments counterattacked with grenades. Consequently, both sides soon became engaged in a vicious close-quarter battle in the mist around the old British front line. The 10th Essex from the 53rd Brigade eventually reinforced the 36th Brigade, giving the attack the momentum necessary to reach the first objective.

At 0620hrs, two hours after the attack commenced, the 12th Division launched a subsidiary operation with the 35th Brigade in front of Morlancourt. The attack was successful in the centre and on the left, capturing 300 men of I and III/124th Infantry Regiment, but was held up on the right.

South of the Somme, the first phase of the Australian Corps' assault annihilated the forward battalions of XI Corps. The German defences in this area were particularly vulnerable owing to the poor disposition of some of their troops and the ongoing relief of the 43rd and 108th divisions. In an attempt to counter the recent Australian raiding, the 13th Division deployed 13 of its companies in the forward zone with only 11 retained for the main defensive position, contrary to their normal doctrine. In the sector immediately south of the river the forward battalions of the 97th Infantry

A German casualty being recovered from the ruins of Sailly-Laurette. By August 1918 the Allied naval blockade had seriously reduced the amount and quality of medical equipment available to the German Army with crepe paper being used to bandage wounds in some cases. Access to the well-equipped Allied medical services gave wounded captives a much better chance of survival than if they had been evacuated by the German system. (IWM Q 6907)

Regiment had relieved the 202nd Infantry Regiment but were still retained under command of the outgoing 202nd Infantry Regiment staff.

The artillery barrage and thick mist stunned and blinded the defenders allowing the brigades of the 2nd and 3rd Australian divisions to push forwards rapidly. In confused conditions many posts were bypassed and subsequently attacked from the flank or rear. The 9th and 11th Australian brigades of the 3rd Australian Division were soon in possession of Gailly Ridge, whilst to their right the 7th and 5th Australian brigades of the 2nd Australian Division captured the villages of Lamotte-Warfusée. As the Australians closed on their objective the mist began to thin allowing the tanks of the 2nd and 13th tank battalions to take a greater part in the action. On the right flank, the 26th (Queensland) Battalion crossed into the Canadian sector and assaulted Marcelcave after coming under fire from there. Farther north, the forward German artillery positions in the valleys running north from Warfusée to the Somme were taken by surprise and captured as the first objective was secured.

The attack of the Canadian Corps struck the northern two divisions of LI Corps. The terrain in this sector was particularly difficult as the valley of the river Luce ran obliquely from the forward right to the rear left of the Canadian advance. Furthermore, as the southernmost corps of Fourth Army, Currie's men were required to liaise with the French XXXI Corps who were to attack on their right 45 minutes after the Canadians moved forwards. To compensate for this, the 3rd Division on the right flank had a motorized machine-gun brigade under Brigadier-General Brutinel, a narrower frontage, greater artillery support and more limited objectives than its neighbours. In order to minimize difficulties in coordinating an assault over the river, 3rd Canadian Division attacked with two brigades forwards, the 9th Canadian, which was deployed across the Luce in the Hourges bridgehead, and the 8th Canadian north of the river. Farther north the 1st and 2nd Canadian divisions each attacked with one brigade in line.

The mist and marshy ground disrupted the cooperation of the tanks and infantry, causing the 9th Canadian Brigade to engage in heavy fighting with the 373rd Infantry Regiment in Rifle Wood. However, after a breakthrough farther to the north around Demuin, tanks were able to outflank and clear Rifle and Harmon woods. The 1st Canadian Division attacked with the 3rd Canadian Brigade who cleared the troops of the 117th Division from the re-entrants north of Hangard Village and Hangard Wood. The tanks of the 4th Tank Battalion scattered the defenders they encountered, but those that were missed offered stiff resistance to the following infantry. As the fighting subsequently spread across the Canadian sector, many dislocated actions took place as the Canadian troops reduced the surviving strongpoints with mortars or tanks in support. The 2nd Canadian Division had an easier time as the more open ground in their sector offered little cover to the troops of the 148th Infantry Regiment from the opening barrage. Little serious resistance was met as the first objective was quickly secured.

XXXI Corps launched the attack of the French First Army at 0505hrs after a 45-minute artillery bombardment. The sudden southwards extension of the assault front by the 42nd and 37th divisions caught the left of the German 225th and 14th Bavarian divisions completely by surprise. Their foremost trenches in Moreuil Wood were quickly overrun and by 0700hrs the French first objective on the eastern edge of the wood was secured. Despite the disarray of LI Corps' defences, the French troops then paused as their covering artillery fell 300m ahead. The XXXI Corps attack extended farther to the south at 0635hrs when the 66th Division launched the northernmost of the two assaults with which it aimed to envelop Moreuil and struck into the 4th and 8th Bavarian infantry regiments.

At 0743hrs the barrage lifted and the second phase of the main French attack began. Attempts by the 42nd Division to envelop Villers-aux-Érables were thwarted by heavy fire from the village and the Bois du Dé 400m to the south. The opposition to the 37th Division on their right also stiffened as the battalions of *zouaves* and *tirailleurs* were forced to clear numerous machine-gun posts in succession as they worked their way towards the Bois de Genonville.

A Mk. V* of the 1st Tank Battalion passes through Hourges on 8 August. In the background is a Mk. IV tank that has had it weapons removed and been converted into a supply vehicle. This was one of several novel methods devised to deliver combat supplies to troops in combat in 1918. (IWM CO 2969)

THE DEFENCE OF CERISY (pp. 36–37)

The defence of Cerisy by companies 3 and 4 of the 97th Infantry Regiment and the Machine Gun Company of the 201st Reserve Infantry Regiment provided the Australians with the stiffest resistance they faced on 8 August. All three subunits were in the German rest camp tucked beneath the steep east bank of the spur running south from Cerisy Village when the Australians reached them. The commander of the 202nd Reserve Infantry Regiment, Major Kuhlwein von Rathenow, and his staff were also in the camp and immediately took charge of the situation. At 0600hrs he roused the infantry and machine-gunners and deployed them along the top of the slope facing west, where they waited nervously in the mist. As the Tasmanians of the 15th (Queensland and Tasmania) Battalion crossed the skyline in front of the Germans, they were hit with a fierce hail of machine-gun fire that drove them back into cover behind the crest.

Tanks of the 8th Tank Battalion then crossed the spur and advanced towards the German position. The first groped its way forwards until it reached the very lip of the slope before it withdrew back into the mist. As the mist cleared a second tank (1) advanced but was less fortunate as it suffered an engine failure and was immediately attacked by the defending Germans.

Following their analysis of the fighting at Cambrai, the German Second Army issued instructions on how its units were to combat the tank threat. A sophisticated concept was developed whereby the tanks were to be separated from their supporting infantry before being attacked by the coordinated action of machine-gun

teams, assault grenadiers and, where possible, light mortar teams. Armed with either the heavy MG 08, (2) or the lighter MG 08-15, the German machine-gunners were directed to fire armour-piercing 'K' ammunition at weak spots in the tank's armour and the vision ports to drive the crew into cover inside the vehicle. Once this had been achieved, the grenadiers would assault with hand grenades. which had 'extra' heads (3) strapped to them for increased explosive effect. These would be placed on the tracks or dropped inside the tank if possible.

The second tank was engaged with these methods by Kuhlwein's men who succeeded in setting it alight and capturing the crew. A third tank (4) then crossed the spur and drove parallel to the German line and was heavily engaged, by the machine-gunners of the 201st Reserve Infantry Regiment and the grenadiers of the 97th Infantry Regiment. It too burst into flames and saw its crew taken prisoner as they 'bailed out'.

Although the resolute troops under Kuhlwein's command held off all attacks to their front, their open left flank was soon exposed by the 13th (New South Wales) Battalion who, together with their supporting tanks, brought the Germans under heavy enfilading fire. With his left flank turned, Kuhlwein reluctantly gave the order to withdraw ay 0920hrs. Despite being driven back, the troops of the 201st Reserve and 97th Infantry regiments proved that, when the British lost the mutual support of a coherent tank and infantry attack, the Germans were more than capable of dealing with the armoured threat in 1918.

In the confusion that reigned following the Allied attack the German commanders struggled to gain accurate information on the state of their forces as they began to deploy their reserves and call in reinforcements for an immediate counterattack.

North of the Somme, Second Army gave orders at 0630hrs that the reserve and resting battalions of the 233rd and 54th reserve divisions immediately to the north of the attack sector were to be moved south along with the 479th Regiment of the 243rd Division to launch a counterattack between Morlancourt and the Somme in LIV Corps' sector. The remainder of the 243rd Division, together with the 26th Reserve Division from the neighbouring Seventeenth Army, were ordered to reinforce XI Corps.

In XI Corps, Kühne alarmed his own reserve, the 107th Division, with orders to travel by lorry to Foucaucourt. The 43rd Reserve Division issued orders to mount an immediate counterattack, deploying III/137th Infantry and I/202nd Reserve Infantry regiments forwards to the Chipilly Spur. The 13th Division ordered the III/15th and I/55th infantry regiments to the eastern edge of the Morcourt Valley, whilst to their rear, I/13th and II/203rd infantry regiments moved forwards to Hill 84. To their left, the 41st Division attempted to form a second line with the I/201st, II/152nd, I/55th and III/15th infantry regiments, as well as two companies of the I/18th Infantry Regiment.

South of the Amiens–Chaulnes railway, Marwitz placed the 109th Division under command of LI Corps and requested that the reserve of the neighbouring Eighteenth Army, the 119th Division, be deployed in the direction of Vrély. The 109th Division began moving forwards to Harbonnières between 0500 and 0600hrs whilst the 119th Division began concentrating its troops, who were out training, prior to advancing towards Caix. At LI Corps, Hofacker incorrectly assumed that the attack would not extend south of the Amiens–Roye road and immediately ordered the withdrawal of the resting battalions of the 14th Bavarian and 192nd divisions on his left in order to reinforce the 225th and 117th divisions on his right.

The unprecedented depth of the Allied penetration on 8 August enabled them to surprise many German regimental commanders at their battle HQs, such as these captured by Canadian troops. (IWM CO 3001)

However, the Bavarians had already moved under the initiative of their own commanders to the south of Mézières. The three resting battalions of the 192nd Division were placed under command of Hauptmann Bellmann (CO III/192nd Infantry Regiment), and temporarily named 'Bellmann's Regiment' before being deployed north to Beaucourt. At the same time LI Corps requested that III Corps on their left move the 1st Reserve Division to the Corps boundary. III Corps agreed immediately and deployed the division into the battle area along the Amiens–Roye road.

The second phase – seizing the guns

Between 0630 and 0800hrs the first wave of the Allied attack secured the majority of their initial objectives. Only in III Corps' sector, where the mist and the efforts of LIV Corps had disrupted the attack, was success elusive. As the first wave dug in, the troops of the second wave moved forwards to their assembly areas and assumed their assault formations. At about this time the mist began to clear, revealing to all the magnitude of the success so far achieved. More importantly, however, it also allowed the German artillery and the RAF to begin to influence the battle.

In III Corps, the 173rd Brigade was to assault the second objective in 58th Division's sector. Unfortunately, owing to the German attack on 6 August none of their officers had been able to conduct a reconnaissance of the proposed advance. The second objective lay on the far side of Gressaire Wood, which was occupied by the III/120th and II/123rd infantry regiments, along with remnants of the front-line garrison who had retreated and the battery positions of the 27th Division's artillery. The 173rd Brigade had moved forwards in the wake of the 174th Brigade but soon lost their way, moving north into the 18th Division's sector. As they struggled back to the north end of Malard Wood they passed through the 174th Brigade to begin their assault. In the clearing conditions the troops of the 3rd Londons and 2/4th Londons were met by a hail of machine-gun fire from Gressaire Wood, and were forced to return to first objective. To their north, the 10th Essex continued the attack of the 18th Division and quickly secured the second objective north-west of Gressaire Wood. They were joined by 7th Royal West Kents, who extended a north-facing flank to the rear left of the Essex. The third battalion of the 53rd Brigade, the 8th Royal Berkshire, moved forwards on the right of the Essex towards Gressaire Wood, however they met the same fate as the Londons to the south and were forced to withdraw in the face of intense machine-gun fire.

Unlike their northern neighbours, the Australian second wave deployed in relative peace following the shattering success of the initial attack. As the mist cleared the 4th and 5th Australian divisions deployed into their assault formations, supported by 84 tanks, from the 2nd, 8th, 13th and 15th tank battalions, 12 cars of the 17th Armoured Car Battalion, six artillery brigades and two heavy gun batteries. The 1st Cavalry Brigade moved forwards on the right flank supported by Whippet tanks.

At 0820hrs the second phase got under way as the Australians moved forwards. In the clearing conditions the tanks immediately began to take on

the role of suppressing enemy strongpoints in the absence of a creeping barrage, whilst the corps squadrons of the RAF began to screen the attack from enemy-held villages and woods with smoke from phosphorous bombs.

In the 5th Australian Division sector the artillery batteries of the 13th, 41st and 117th divisions around Bayonvillers and Wiencourt provided the focus for the German defence. Having pulled their guns out of their pits in order to engage the Australians over open sights, the German gunners destroyed several tanks and caused some casualties to the leading troops of the 15th and 8th brigades. However, working in close cooperation, the infantry and the tanks were soon able to manoeuvre around the flanks of each battery in succession and capture them. Despite the tank losses, the advance maintained a rapid pace with Bayonvillers quickly captured as surprised German parties departed in haste.

As the 15th Australian Brigade approached Bayonvillers, the leading squadrons of the 1st Cavalry Brigade passed through the Australian ranks and, sweeping north and south of the village, pushed on towards Harbonnières attacking isolated German troops and transport as they tried to withdraw.

To the north, the 12th Australian Brigade of the 4th Australian Division rapidly crossed the valleys running south from Cerisy and Morcourt, capturing 13 batteries of the 13th, 43rd Reserve and 108th divisions on the way. As the Australians approached the Morcourt Valley they came under fire from the defensive positions hastily occupied by I/201st and II/152nd infantry regiments, two companies of the I/18th Infantry Regiment and the I/26th Company of Engineers and took cover. The steepness of the valley prevented assistance from the tanks as the first one to attempt the descent rolled over. However, at this point the cars of the 17th Armoured Car Battalion passed through the advancing infantry and headed into the German rear areas along the Roman road. In doing so they passed across the left flank of the German positions, raking them with machine-gun fire before pressing on towards Foucaucourt. Furthermore, a battery of field artillery was able to take up position and open fire on the defenders. Under the covering fire of these two units, the 46th (Victoria) and 30th (New South Wales) battalions were able to advance by short rushes to the valley on either side of the Roman road and break into the positions of the II/152nd Infantry Regiment who withdrew. The troops of the 46th were then able to turn their attack to the north in order to suppress the I/201st Infantry Regiment who were firing at the advancing 45th (New South Wales) Battalion. The troops of the I/18th Infantry Regiment who were not engaged, seeing the British cavalry on their southern flank panicked and began to withdraw in disorder.

The success in the Australian centre along the Roman road assisted the 4th Australian Brigade who met the strongest opposition faced by the Australian Corps on this day. The brigade attacked with three battalions in line during the second phase. The 14th (Victoria) Battalion in the centre immediately came under fire from a machine-gun nest on the forward slope of the ridge south of Cerisy, which was assaulted in concert with the accompanying tanks. On their left the 15th (Queensland and Tasmania) Battalion was led into

Austin armoured cars of the 17th Armoured Car Battalion moving along the Roman road. The Austin had a 30hp engine which gave a top speed of 56km/ph. Each of its twin turrets was armed with a single Hotchkiss machine gun and it had armour plate up to 6mm thick. A design peculiarity of this vehicle was a rear-facing driving position. (IWM E(Aus) 3099)

Cerisy by six tanks; however, the narrow defile between the steep riverbank and the Somme caused the tanks to withdraw back through the village and attempt to climb the ridge south of Cerisy from the west. As the 14th continued their advance over the crest of the ridge they came under fire from two companies of the I/97th Infantry Regiment and the machine-gun companies of the 201st and 202nd infantry regiments. Attempts to launch another combined attack with the tanks were thwarted as Monash's fears about the vulnerability of his left flank were realized. In the clearing conditions, German batteries in Celestins Wood and Chipilly swung round to their left and began to engage the advancing Australians, quickly destroying several tanks.

The right of the 14th (Victoria) Battalion was also pinned down by machine-gun fire from the I/55th Infantry Regiment, who by this time had occupied a sunken lane on the east side of the Morcourt Valley. The 39th Battery, supporting the Australians, galloped into action and fired 100 shells into the Germans, allowing the 14th (Victoria) Battalion to move into Morcourt from the south. Seeing their left flank turned, the party from I/97th Infantry Regiment in Cerisy abandoned their position and withdrew along the riverbank.

The 13th (New South Wales) Battalion had met little opposition up to this point, but as they moved into the Morcourt Valley they were engaged by the remnants of the I/55th Infantry Regiment, by III/15th Infantry Regiment, who had moved forwards, and by artillery fire from north of the Somme. Despite this they were steadied by CSM Oswald who led them across the valley to the second objective.

The artillery duel with the German guns north of the Somme became intense as more Australian batteries took up position after moving forwards. Ignoring orders not to fire over the Somme into III Corps' sector, a section of the 38th Battery began to fire at the guns on the Chipilly Spur. It was quickly ranged by the Germans who destroyed it after they had fired only two shells per gun. The German guns from the 8th Battery, 13th Field Artillery Regiment, continued to harass the Australians between the Somme and the Roman road as they completed their advance to the second objective.

An 18-pdr battery in action. The 18-pdr was the main weapon of the field artillery in the divisional artillery brigades, equipping three of the four batteries in each brigade. It was brought into service in 1904 and by 1918 the Mk. III variant had a range of 8,230m. (IWM E(Aus) 2925)

The view from the position of 8th Battery, 13th Field Artillery Regiment, in Celestins Wood south-west across the Somme valley as the mist burns away on an August morning. The village of Cerisy is in the foreground with Susan Wood on the skyline to the left and Reginald Wood on the skyline to the right. The German gunners harried the 4th Australian Brigade as they advanced across the fields between Cerisy and the woods. (Author's collection)

The Canadian assault moved on remorselessly as the attack of the 7th Canadian Brigade, on the right, met with minimal German resistance and was described as, 'a route march enlivened by the sight of enemy running in every direction'. Progress was rapid and the second objective was secured at 1000hrs. In the centre, the battalions of the 1st Canadian Brigade faced slightly stiffer opposition from scattered machine guns concealed in crops and small woods. These were dealt with by the infantry themselves, who reached their objective and cleared Cayeaux by 1130hrs. The 5th Canadian Brigade fought through the strongest resistance faced by the Canadians in the second phase. Tanks from the 14th Tank Battalion outflanked artillery positions of the 117th and 41st divisions west of Wiencourt from the south. The 24th (Victoria Rifles of Canada) and 26th (New Brunswick) battalions then assaulted the three resting battalions of the 117th Division, which had occupied the hill east of Guillaucourt. After a short fight the second objective was taken.

In order to exploit the successful break-in the French First Army extended its operations to the right and attempted to expand its original break-in. XXXI Corps introduced 153rd Division in between the 42nd and 37th divisions whilst the right of 66th Division commenced the envelopment of Moreuil from the south. To the right of XXXI Corps, IX Corps began their assault over the Avre to cover the advance of their northern neighbour.

Although 42nd Division completed the capture of Villers-aux-Érables by 0945hrs, resistance continued in the Bois du Dé to the south and Mézières to the east. As a consequence the 42nd Division was faced with the difficult prospect of conducting a forward passage of lines with 153rd Division at the same time as they maintained their own advance in contact with the 14th Bavarian Division. Between 1000 and 1030hrs the leading elements of the 153rd Division reached the western edge of Villers-aux-Érables, but due to heavy fire from Mézières and the Bois du Dé were forced to the north into the 42nd Division's sector, which was trying to outflank Mézières from the north. To the south, the 37th Division secured its second objectives in the Bois de Genonville and the Bois de Touffu by 0930hrs where it then halted to deploy the second echelon battalions for the advance to Plessier.

The attack of IX Corps met stiff resistance from the 14th Bavarian and 192nd divisions. The Avre Valley was up to 600m wide at this point with broad expanses of marsh crossed by only a limited number of routes. Heavy machine-gun fire from the Bois de Genonville and Genonville Farm decimated the ranks of the 15th Colonial Division as they attempted to cross at 0820hrs, with only tenuous gains made on the far bank. On the right of the corps sector the 3rd Division was more successful. Using smokescreens as cover, two crossing points were established south of La Neuville and Hill 82 was seized by 0905hrs. The remainder of the Division followed up quickly and began to push forwards to the east and south-east.

The third phase – driving on to the Amiens Defence Line
The third phase saw the continuation of the assaults by the Australian and Canadian corps that penetrated the German defences to a depth unprecedented in Allied operations on the Western Front.

A Mk. V 'male' tank passing a Canadian field ambulance in Hangard on 8 August. The modified wide tracks fitted to Mk. Vs are clearly visible on the photograph together with the 'white–red–white' recognition marking on the roof hatch of the command cab. (IWM CO 2967)

The Australians continued their mercurial performance with notable contributions by the 1st Cavalry Brigade, the 17th Armoured Car Company and the RAF. Simultaneously, the corps conducted a prolonged engagement with the surviving German artillery on the Chipilly Spur.

The regiments of the 1st Cavalry Brigade began to pass through the leading lines of infantry between the first and second objective around Harbonnières. The 2nd and 5th Dragoon Guards galloped eastwards, passing the town to both the north and south. A large railway gun was seen on the tracks to the north of Harbonnières as it fired un-aimed shots to the west. As the gun crew attempted to withdraw the gun by train, they came under attack by two aircraft which managed to disable the engine. A squadron of the 5th Dragoon Guards arrived on the scene, captured the gun and sent the panic-stricken Germans retreating to Vauvillers. The troopers then pushed forwards to Vauvillers and Framerville to cover the advance of the infantry to the third objective behind them.

The 17th Armoured Car Battalion had driven even farther into the German rear having passed through the infantry earlier in the day. The battalion advanced east along the Roman road and then split into three parties. The first headed south to Framerville where a German HQ was raided and transport wagons shot up. The cars continued through the village attacking infantry and artillery teams before returning to the Roman road. The second group headed north to Proyart where unsuspecting German troops were machine-gunned through the windows of their billets as they sat at breakfast. The cars then drove farther north to Chuignolles where a German machine-gun company was engaged in a firefight prior to the cars' returning towards the Roman road. The third group advanced to Foucaucourt, where they were engaged by field guns and found the road blocked by fugitive German transport. This party too reversed course back to the third objective.

The cavalry and armoured cars covered the 4th and 5th Australian divisions as they advanced towards the third objective. As they did so they met the leading elements of the German reinforcements arriving on the battlefield.

The 376th and 2nd Grenadier regiments of the 109th Division reached their assembly area south-east of Harbonnières at 0915hrs. The senior officer

in this sector was Generalmajor Hoefer, commander of the 117th Division. Receiving no orders from XI Corps, Hoefer directed I and II/376th Infantry Regiment south of the railway to face the Canadians and ordered II/2nd Grenadier Regiment to hold Harbonnières.

Assuming that there was little organized defence in front of them the 8th and 15th Australian brigades commenced their advance without waiting for their tank support to arrive, although the armour soon caught up to assist the assault on Harbonnières. As they attempted to advance east of the village they ran into two companies of II/2nd Grenadier Regiment approaching from the opposite direction who, seeing tanks and infantry advancing from the eastern edge of the village, immediately engaged with machine-gun and trench mortar fire, destroying the tanks and driving the infantry back into the village.

Shortly afterwards, reconnaissance aircraft alerted the Australians to the proximity of the 109th Division to the east. By now the command staff of the 109th Division had reached the area and was ordered to secure a line from north-east of Harbonnières to Cayeux. Orders were issued for the 26th Reserve Regiment and II/2nd Grenadier Regiment to attack north of Harbonnières with the remainder of 2nd Grenadier Regiment and III/376th Infantry Regiment attacking to the south. However, events had already overtaken the 109th as two battalions were already engaged around Vauvillers. The remainder were brought to a halt on the Amiens Defence Line by effective artillery and machine-gun fire, where they remained for the rest of the day.

I and II/376th Infantry Regiment had fared little better. Shortly after crossing the Amiens–Chaulnes railway they had been assailed from the air and on the ground by cavalry and Whippet tanks around Guillaucourt. They were swiftly broken as an effective force and retreated along with the remnants of the 117th Division.

North of the Roman road, the troops of the 4th Australian Division had a much tougher battle. By coincidence the remnants of the German front-line divisions had formed a hasty defence line along the third objective between Proyart and Méricourt, whilst the German artillery on the Chipilly Spur, north of the Somme, remained a persistent threat to the left flank. Only two Australian battalions were used in the advance, the 16th and the 48th. Immediately north of the Roman road, the 48th (South Australia and Western Australia) Battalion was forced to advance into heavy machine-gun fire from troops of I/148th and II/203rd infantry regiments in the old Amiens Outer Defences. Having taken many casualties, the attack seemed close to failure when the nearest Germans stood up with their hands raised. The Australians swarmed forwards into the German positions and worked their way north with bomb and Lewis gun until they had secured the line up to the copse on Hill 84.

A Canadian 60-pdr gun battery preparing to move forwards at the end of the first phase. The 60-pdr was brought into service in 1904 after experience gained in the Boer War in order to provide a mobile heavy artillery capability. It had a range of 11,247m. (IWM CO 2979)

The view from Hill 95 looking north-west along the Avre Valley. The Avre runs through the trees in the left middle distance, behind which is Genonville Farm. Genonville Wood is on the skyline to the right. The 6th Colonial Infantry Regiment attacked here on 8 August, taking most of the day to overcome the defenders of the 183rd Infantry Regiment of the 192nd Division. (Author's collection)

The 16th (Western Australia and South Australia) Battalion had the toughest task of the day with part of II/203rd and I/13th infantry regiments occupying Hill 84, and detachments of various specialist troops and groups of survivors from the forward battalions extending the line down to the Somme at Méricourt. The attack was spearheaded by a troop of tanks, which first cleared German stragglers between the second and third objectives. Although all the tanks were put out of action, machine-gun teams dismounted and suppressed German troops on the third objective, allowing the companies of the 16th to storm the final line. Having made contact with the 48th on their right, the men of the 16th took cover from the shelling across the Somme in old trenches and gun pits.

At the same time as the third objective was secured, the artillery duel that had begun during the second phase of the attack raged on. The 11th Howitzer Battery and the 37th, 38th and 39th batteries all turned their guns on the batteries of the 13th and 243rd artillery regiments in and around Malard Wood and Chipilly. The German response was rapid and accurate as shells landed amongst the Australian gun teams. The infantry of the 15th (Queensland and Tasmania) Battalion joined the fray by working machine-gun and Lewis gun teams forwards to engage the German batteries, driving the gunners into shelter. The combined efforts of the Australian artillery and infantry began to take effect and, by 1245hrs, the German gunners had withdrawn.

Between 1500 and 1600hrs the leading elements of the 107th Division began to arrive on the battlefield. Having made their way from Péronne by lorry, the 227th and 232nd reserve infantry regiments dismounted less than a kilometre east of Foucaucourt and continued their move on foot. Having been ordered to capture as much ground as possible west of Foucaucourt, they advanced either side of the Roman road until they came under shell and machine-gun fire from the forward Australian positions. The 227th Reserve Infantry Regiment formed a line between the Roman road and Framerville, whilst the 232nd Reserve Infantry Regiment advanced to Proyart. At this point they met with troops of the 478th Infantry Regiment, who formed the leading echelon of the 243rd Division deploying south of the Somme. This regiment was placed under command of the 108th Division and was joined by its sister, the 122nd Infantry Regiment at 2100hrs. Together the 107th and 108th divisions formed a new line from Framerville to Proyart and linked to the forces remaining between Hill 84 and Méricourt.

During the third phase Currie maintained the strength of his right flank by committing the 4th Canadian Division and the 3rd Cavalry Division to the battle through the line held by the 3rd Canadian Division. On his left, the 1st and 2nd Canadian divisions continued their advance with the right of the 1st Cavalry Division supporting the Canadian left.

The Canadian Cavalry Brigade moved forwards on the right with 16 Whippet tanks of the 3rd Tank Battalion. Having gained touch with the French on their right, the brigade then captured 300 Germans in Beaucourt Village. However, attempts to continue the advance on Beaucourt Wood were stopped by a hail of fire from 'Bellmann's Regiment' who occupied it. The 7th Cavalry Brigade on the left was unable to coordinate its attacks effectively with its company of Whippets. Despite this difficulty however, the brigade was able to rush Cayeaux Wood capturing an artillery battery and a large number of machine guns and troops. At 1300hrs the 7th Cavalry Brigade was ordered to continue the advance to the third objective supported on the left by the 6th Cavalry Brigade, which moved forwards from reserve. By 1435hrs the 7th Cavalry Brigade was on the final objective between Caix and Le Quesnel.

The 11th and 12th Canadian brigades of the 4th Canadian Division had moved forwards on the heels of the 3rd Canadian Division. As soon as the second objective was gained they completed their final preparations and were ready to move at 1030hrs. However, Currie's plan envisaged a pause while the cavalry moved forwards. As a result the infantry waited until 1210hrs before they began to advance. In the intervening period, the leading units of the 1st Reserve Division were able to deploy astride the Amiens–Roye road between 1130hrs and 1230hrs.

The 1st Tank Battalion spearheaded the Canadian advance; it was to take the machine-gun teams forwards to the third objective and then return to support the infantry battalions as they advanced. As the ten tanks of A Company approached Le Quesnel they were engaged at close range by concealed field guns supporting the 1st and 59th infantry regiments and nine were destroyed. The battalions of the 11th and 12th Canadian brigades soon

The German 14in. gun captured at Harbonnières by the 1st Cavalry and 8th Australian brigades on 8 August. This gun fired a 700kg shell to a range of 30,000m and posed a major threat to the Amiens rail junction. After the war it was taken to Australia as a trophy where it can be seen today at the Australian War Memorial at Canberra. (IWM E(Aus) 2780)

BRITISH FORCES

173rd Brigade
1 2/4th Londons

4th Australian Brigade
2 13th (New South Wales) Battalion
3 14th (Victoria) Battalion
4 15th (Queensland and Tasmania) Battalion
5 16th (Western Australia and South
   Australia) Battalion

12th Australian Brigade
6 45th (New South Wales) Battalion
7 48th (South Australia and Western
   Australia) Battalion
8 46th (Victoria) Battalion

9 39th Battery Royal Artillery
10 17th Armoured Car Battalion
11 IX Brigade, RAF
12 22nd (Army) Wing, RAF

III ☒ XXX
BUTLER

AUS ☒ XXX
MONASH

MALARD WOOD

CHIPILLY SPUR

CERISY

CHIPILLY

MORCOURT

EVENTS

1 0745–0830hrs: I/13th, III/15th, I/55th, II/97th, III/137th, II/152nd, I/201st Reserve, I/202nd Reserve and II/203rd Reserve infantry regiments ordered forward from rest areas to form a new defence line.

2 0820hrs: lead units of 12th Australian, 4th Australian and 173rd brigades cross the Green Line to commence the second phase. The 2/4 Londons attack immediately halted by shrapnel and machine-gun fire from Chipilly Spur and Gressaire Wood.

3 0830hrs: the I/55th, I/97th and II/97th infantry regiments halt the 13th, 14th and 15th battalions' advance with heavy machine-gun fire.

4 0845hrs: batteries from the 13th, 137th and 243rd field artillery regiments engage the Australians across the Somme from the Chipilly Spur. The tanks closest to the river in support of the 15th (Queensland and Tasmania) Battalion are destroyed.

5 0830–0930hrs: British and Australian artillery push forward to support the assault.

6 0900hrs: 39th Battery RA suppresses I/55th Infantry Regiment allowing 14th (Victoria) Battalion to assault Morcourt from the south. 0920hrs: fearing envelopment the 3 and 4/97th Infantry Regiment withdraw from Cerisy.

7 0930hrs: The 17th Armoured Car Battalion passes through the 46th (Victoria) Battalion, machine-guns Germans in the Morcourt Valley and drives through into German rear. 1000hrs: the 46th (Victoria) Battalion attacks II/152nd Infantry Regiment and then turns north to outflank I/201st Reserve Infantry Regiment.

8 0930hrs onwards: the mist clears allowing 22 (Army) Wing, V Brigade, RAF, to provide close air support to assaulting troops and attack German reinforcements en route to the front. IX Brigade, RAF, conducts high-level patrols to cover 22 (Army) Wing below.

9 1055hrs: 48th (South Australia and Western Australia) and 16th (Western Australia and South Australia) battalions begin the third phase. 1230hrs: the 48th (South Australia and Western Australia) Battalion assault and clear the Amiens Defence Line as far as the copse on Hill 84. The 16th (Western Australia and South Australia) Battalion reaches its final objective but withdraws to a less exposed position.

CHIPILLY SPUR: 8 AUGUST

Second and third phases of attack viewed from the south-east. Despite the near annihilation of its divisions south of the Somme, the defence of the Chipilly Spur by XI Corps exposed the left flank of the Australian Corps and prevented Monash from exploiting his success.

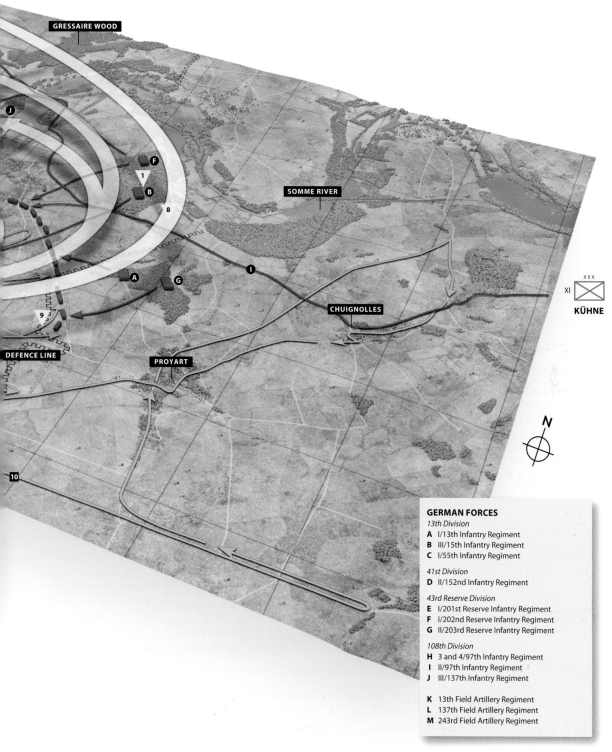

Note: Gridlines are shown at intervals of 1km/0.62miles

GRESSAIRE WOOD

J

F

1

B

8

SOMME RIVER

A

G

I

CHUIGNOLLES

9

DEFENCE LINE

PROYART

10

XI

xxx

KÜHNE

N

GERMAN FORCES

13th Division
A I/13th Infantry Regiment
B III/15th Infantry Regiment
C I/55th Infantry Regiment

41st Division
D II/152nd Infantry Regiment

43rd Reserve Division
E I/201st Reserve Infantry Regiment
F I/202nd Reserve Infantry Regiment
G II/203rd Reserve Infantry Regiment

108th Division
H 3 and 4/97th Infantry Regiment
I II/97th Infantry Regiment
J III/137th Infantry Regiment

K 13th Field Artillery Regiment
L 137th Field Artillery Regiment
M 243rd Field Artillery Regiment

51

followed up the tank attack and were quickly embroiled with 'Bellmann's Regiment' in Beaucourt Wood. North of the wood, 12th Canadian Brigade swept away III/183rd Infantry Regiment on Bellmann's right flank and threatened to envelop his whole force. Weakened after hard fighting, Bellmann ordered his troops to withdraw to the Caix–Le Quesnel road. Exhausted by their efforts, the Canadians halted their advance at 1630hrs on the southern edge of the wood, 2,500m short of their final objective.

On the Canadian left, the 9th Cavalry Brigade moved forwards supported by Whippets of the 6th Tank Battalion soon after 1100hrs. Aerial reconnaissance identified total confusion in the German lines between Guillaucourt and Rosières and the 15th and 19th Hussars swept forwards to take advantage. By 1300hrs they had occupied the third objective and were in touch with the 1st Cavalry Brigade on their right. The 2nd Cavalry Brigade was then moved forwards from reserve to occupy the gap between the 9th and 7th cavalry brigades.

The 7th and 10th battalions of the 2nd Canadian Brigade began their advance around noon and, finding the ground cleared of enemy by the preceding cavalry, occupied the third objective by 1430hrs. Farther north, the final assault wave of the 2nd Canadian Division slowly made its way forwards and only crossed the second objective at 1630hrs. On the infantry's arrival at the third objective the troops of the 2nd and 9th cavalry brigades were relieved and withdrawn.

The 119th Division began their move to the battle area by lorry at 1030hrs. They came under repeated attacks from RAF that greatly hindered their progress. The leading regiment arrived in Vrély at 1300hrs with the last pulling in at 1930hrs. Placed under the command of LI Corps, they were ordered to mount a counterattack with 192nd Division to re-establish a line between Harbonnières and Le Quesnel. Without maps, without knowing the ground and disrupted by the delayed arrival of the troops, the attack lacked conviction and was brought to a halt by Canadian fire east of Caix. The 119th then formed a new line between Rosières and Le Quesnel between the 109th and 1st Reserve divisions.

A 'Whippet' tank passing Canadian soldiers digging in on the second objective. The spare petrol cans seen draped on the side of the cab were a significant vulnerability as they were prone to ignite under German defensive fire. (IWM CO 2974)

Although no attacks were planned for III Corps in this phase, the 58th Division mounted a second attack in an effort to cover the Australians to the south. Confusion over the possibility of British troops being in Chipilly caused the covering bombardment to be cancelled. Predictably, at 1500hrs when the 2/2nd Londons advanced they were lashed by machine-gun fire from Chipilly Spur and Gressaire Wood and were soon driven back to their start point.

At the same time, the reserves of the 233rd and 54th reserve divisions were moving into two concentration areas in preparation for their counterattack against III Corps. The first group commanded by Major Gutscher consisted of I/248th Reserve, III/246th Infantry and II/450th Infantry regiments and was placed at the disposal of 54th Reserve Division. The second group, commanded by Oberstleutnant Lägeler, included III/247th Reserve, III/248th Reserve and two companies of III/124th Infantry regiments and was placed under command of the 27th Division. The objective was the sector between Morlancourt and the Bray–Corbie road and the assault was launched between 1430 and 1515hrs. Heavy air and artillery attacks caused numerous casualties as the Germans advanced. However, the forward positions of III Corps east of the crossroads, held by the 10th Essex, became increasingly exposed and were withdrawn to the first objective allowing the German line to be re-established west of the Morlancourt–Chipilly road by 1630hrs. The third regiment of the 243rd Division, the 479th Infantry Regiment, arrived at Bray at 1600hrs. Placed under the command of the 27th Division, III/479th Infantry Regiment moved forwards to the area of Gressaire Wood and suffered under heavy air attacks on the way arriving at 1900hrs. Meanwhile, I/479th Infantry Regiment remained in Bray as the divisional reserve.

The combined forces of the French 42nd and 153rd divisions cleared the final Bavarian defenders out of Mézières and the Bois du Dé almost simultaneously. As a preparatory bombardment was being fired on Mézières, troops of both divisions noted a lack of defensive fire coming from the village. Realizing that the village was unoccupied by the Germans they quickly moved

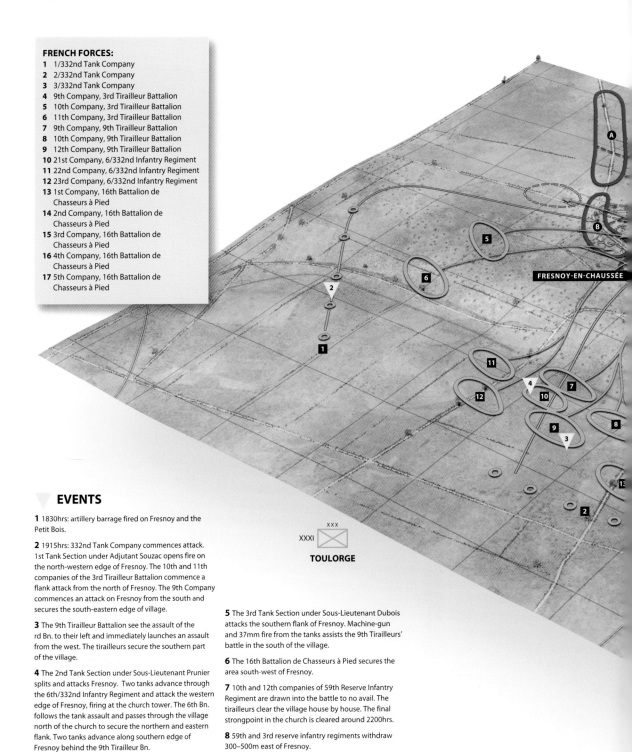

FRESNOY-EN-CHAUSSÉE

EVENTS

1 1830hrs: artillery barrage fired on Fresnoy and the Petit Bois.

2 1915hrs: 332nd Tank Company commences attack. 1st Tank Section under Adjutant Souzac opens fire on the north-western edge of Fresnoy. The 10th and 11th companies of the 3rd Tirailleur Battalion commence a flank attack from the north of Fresnoy. The 9th Company commences an attack on Fresnoy from the south and secures the south-eastern edge of village.

3 The 9th Tirailleur Battalion see the assault of the rd Bn. to their left and immediately launches an assault from the west. The tirailleurs secure the southern part of the village.

4 The 2nd Tank Section under Sous-Lieutenant Prunier splits and attacks Fresnoy. Two tanks advance through the 6th/332nd Infantry Regiment and attack the western edge of Fresnoy, firing at the church tower. The 6th Bn. follows the tank assault and passes through the village north of the church to secure the northern and eastern flank. Two tanks advance along southern edge of Fresnoy behind the 9th Tirailleur Bn.

XXX
XXXI
TOULORGE

5 The 3rd Tank Section under Sous-Lieutenant Dubois attacks the southern flank of Fresnoy. Machine-gun and 37mm fire from the tanks assists the 9th Tirailleurs' battle in the south of the village.

6 The 16th Battalion de Chasseurs à Pied secures the area south-west of Fresnoy.

7 10th and 12th companies of 59th Reserve Infantry Regiment are drawn into the battle to no avail. The tirailleurs clear the village house by house. The final strongpoint in the church is cleared around 2200hrs.

8 59th and 3rd reserve infantry regiments withdraw 300–500m east of Fresnoy.

ATTACK OF FRENCH XXXI CORPS AT FRESNOY-EN-CHAUSSÉE: 1915HRS 8 AUGUST 1918

Having captured Mézières earlier in the afternoon, the 42nd and 153rd divisions continued their advance until 1600hrs, when they reached Fresnoy-en-Chaussée, occupied by 1st Reserve Division and the remnants of 14th Bavarian Division in Lüttwitz' III Corps.

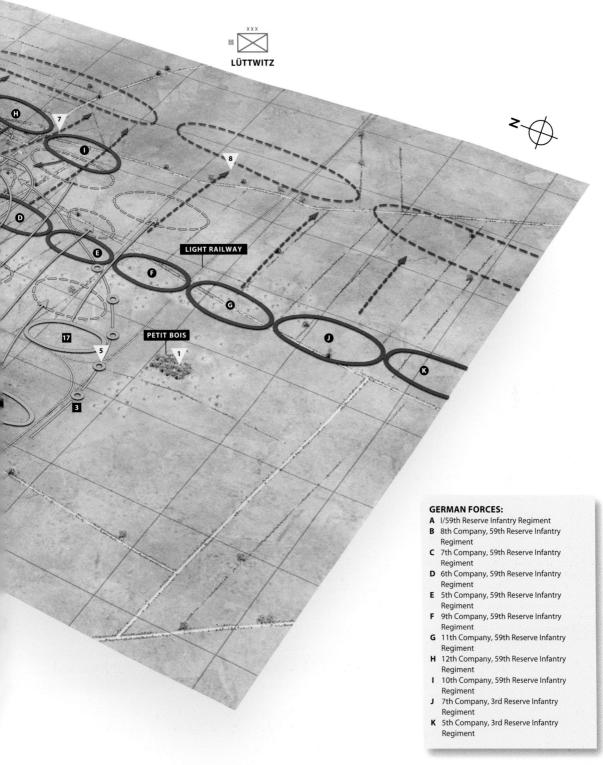

Note: Gridlines are shown at intervals of 250m/273yds

LÜTTWITZ

LIGHT RAILWAY

PETIT BOIS

GERMAN FORCES:

A I/59th Reserve Infantry Regiment
B 8th Company, 59th Reserve Infantry Regiment
C 7th Company, 59th Reserve Infantry Regiment
D 6th Company, 59th Reserve Infantry Regiment
E 5th Company, 59th Reserve Infantry Regiment
F 9th Company, 59th Reserve Infantry Regiment
G 11th Company, 59th Reserve Infantry Regiment
H 12th Company, 59th Reserve Infantry Regiment
I 10th Company, 59th Reserve Infantry Regiment
J 7th Company, 3rd Reserve Infantry Regiment
K 5th Company, 3rd Reserve Infantry Regiment

forwards and secured it. At the same time, the 42nd Division raked the Bois du Dé with fire from Villers-aux-Érables, and attacked from the west in conjunction with the 326th Tank Company. After a stiff fight, the wood was captured shortly before midday.

At this point the attack of XXXI Corps began to lose momentum as the 42nd and 153rd divisions attempted to disentangle themselves, bring forward their artillery and secure their respective objectives of Fresnoy-en-Chaussée and Hangest. Leading elements of the 153rd Division continued to advance on Hangest but at 1400hrs machine-gun fire halted them 300m to the west of Fresnoy, where they were joined at around 1530hrs by the 42nd Division. Their supporting artillery batteries had occupied their new positions between Villers-aux-Érables and Mézières by 1400hrs; however, due to the inability to deliver ammunition to them, their rate of fire was greatly reduced to conserve their stocks. To compensate for this, the 332nd Tank Company was detailed to support the 42nd Division's attack on Fresnoy.

Despite the frantic urging from their commander, 42nd Division's troops could not deliver their attack before 1930hrs. Meanwhile, the 153rd Division had decided independently to attack Fresnoy in order to secure their left flank as they advanced on Hangest. However, shortly before the artillery barrage in support of the attack on Hangest opened at 1830hrs, both divisions became aware of each other's intentions. Unable to disentangle the two plans at this late stage the troops simply decided to move when the artillery opened fire.

The combined assault was launched at 1830hrs when the barrage fell on the German positions. Supported by the 332nd Tank Company, the French infantry enveloped Fresnoy from north and south. Once the attack had broken into the village a vicious close-quarter battle developed as the attackers fought from house to house with rifles, bayonets and grenades to clear the defenders from their positions. By 2230hrs the village was secure.

To the south, in IX Corps sector, the 192nd Division continued to resist the efforts of 15th Colonial and 3rd divisions around Genonville Farm, Hill 95 and Braches. However, by late morning the leading elements of the 37th Division were beginning to close in on Plessier and threatening to cut off the 192nd Division from the north. Those defenders that could withdrew to Plessier, forming a new line facing north-west, opening the way for the stalled attack of the 15th Colonial Division. At 1140hrs, Genonville Farm was captured and the advance resumed. The Africans took the remainder of the day to clear the rearguards of the 192nd Division from their positions, with the Bois de Genonville being secured by 1500hrs and Hill 95 soon after. By 1945hrs the 15th Colonial Division had taken all its objectives. On their right the 3rd Division continued to push into the right flank of the 24th Division but were met with fierce resistance. Contact was made with the 37th Division at Plessier but to the south-east the division could advance no farther than the western edge of the Bois de St Hubert.

Assault from the air

The RAF played a significant role in the day's fighting, particularly with close support and interdiction missions. Although the misty conditions prevented the surprise attack on the German aerodromes, from the second phase of the attack onwards the air battle was intense. In addition to laying smokescreens to cover the infantry, the German reserves were severely disrupted as they attempted to join the battle. The aircraft of V Brigade swarmed over the battlefield, attacking bodies of troops wherever they were found with machine guns and bombs. Hasty defensive positions formed by the remnants of front-line divisions were attacked to enable the tanks and infantry to close in, whilst all the divisions hurrying to the front from north-east and south were repeatedly forced from the road by attacks.

Despite these successes, the air battle changed character dramatically in the afternoon. Late in the morning the aircrews noted that the approach roads to the Somme crossings were becoming choked with retreating troops and transport. Sensing an opportunity to trap a large number of German troops west of the river, and prevent reinforcements moving into the battle area, Major-General Salmond cancelled existing orders and directed a massed attack on the Somme bridges. The bridge at Brie was attacked repeatedly by aircraft of 54, 107 and 205 squadrons. The Péronne road and rail bridges were attacked by 1, 43 and 98 squadrons whilst the bridge at Béthancourt was attacked twice by 49 and 32 squadrons. 27 and 73 squadrons attacked the bridges at Voyennes, Pithon and Offoy.

The attacks at Béthancourt met the first signs of the German response in the air. The Jastas attached to Second and Eighteenth armies had begun scoring sporadically around 0900hrs as the mist cleared. However, in an attempt to enable German ground-attack and observation aircraft to operate effectively, the Jastas were ordered to abandon high-level patrols and concentrate their strength at lower altitudes around midday where they met the incoming RAF raids. Of the 22 aircraft in the first raid only seven reached Béthancourt. In the second raid, the 18 RAF aircraft were intercepted just as they commenced their attack with the result that no accurate bombing was possible.

Reinforcements began to reach Second Army in the afternoon as Sixth, Ninth, Seventeenth and Eighteenth armies dispatched 86 fighters, 19 ground-attack aircraft, 16 bombers and 57 support aircraft. These included elements from the elite *Jagdgeschwader* who were ordered north to join the battle from their bases in Champagne. Oberstleutnant Erich Löwenhardt led the veterans of JG I into the fray and by the end of the day had seen his unit claim 13 victims.

Order, counter-order, disorder

The results of the day's fighting were remarkable. The Fourth Army had advanced to a depth of 13km on a 14km front. For around 9,000 of their own casualties, the Fourth Army had inflicted around 23,500 on the Germans, including 12,000 prisoners, and captured over 400 artillery pieces. The French First Army had captured 3,500 prisoners. In the process, six German divisions had been virtually wiped out.

However, key elements of the Allied armoury had suffered heavy casualties during the day, particularly the RAF and Tank Corps. Of the aircraft committed to battle, 45 were lost and 52 others removed from squadron strength because of damage. Of these 70 were from the squadrons attacking the bridges and ground targets, representing 23 per cent of that force. Only 155 tanks were available for action the next day, the remainder having been destroyed, damaged or their crews incapacitated.

As the extent of the Allied gains became apparent, Haig exhorted Rawlinson and Debeney to push on. At 1130hrs he requested that Debeney commit the French II Cavalry Corps to support the British cavalry in extending the breakthrough. Unfortunately, Debeney could not comply as II Cavalry Corps had been deployed behind his right flank with XXXV Corps at Montdidier, rather than on his left with XXXI Corps. Worse still for Haig,

Renault FT 17 tanks of the 11th Tank Battalion advance past a 75mm gun battery to assault Fresnoy on 8 August. The FT 17 was first used in action in May 1918. It had 16mm thick armour on the front and turret of the vehicle and 8mm thick elsewhere. The major drawback was endurance, as four of its 83 litres of fuel were consumed every mile by its 35hp engine. (IWM Q 56452)

Debeney's orders for 9 August were couched in an equivocal tone. Although XXXI Corps was given objectives to be gained, IX and X Corps were only tasked with covering the right of XXXI Corps whilst XXXV Corps' attack was delayed to take place on orders rather than begin at the original planned time.

Meanwhile Haig's direction to Rawlinson was to push forwards to the Roye–Chaulnes line with his main effort directed towards Roye on the right. Rawlinson began by moving his reserve divisions forwards. The 32nd Division was moved to Domart behind the Canadian Corps; the 17th Division was concentrated 11km east of Amiens behind the Australian Corps, whilst the 63rd Division assembled west of Albert behind III Corps. At 1600hrs Rawlinson visited Currie and agreed that the 32nd Division would be released to the Canadian Corps. The advance would continue with the 32nd Division on the right with 1st and 2nd Canadian divisions in the centre and left. This attack would be preceded by the capture of Le Quesnel by 4th Canadian Division. Currie set the time for the start of the attack at 0500hrs the following morning. Orders to this effect were prepared, but at 1830hrs just prior to their issue, a telegram was received from Fourth Army HQ reversing the decision to commit 32nd Division to the Canadians.

The OHL's initial reaction continued in the same complacent manner that had characterized the preceding weeks. Failing to grasp the now-parlous state of the Second Army, Ludendorff demanded that the situation be restored by counterattacks by 107th, 119th and 1st Reserve divisions, informing the Kaiser later in the afternoon that he would launch an enveloping attack at the northern and southern flanks of the breakthrough 'like Cambrai in 1917'. Consequently, the OHL and Heeresgruppe Rupprecht began to move reserves into concentration areas west of Péronne and north-west of Roye. From the north the 38th Division arrived at Chaulnes in the early morning of the 9th whilst the 21st and 5th Bavarian divisions, together with the Alpenkorps were expected later in the day. From the south, two regiments of the 82nd Reserve Division reinforced the 24th and 1st reserve divisions whilst the 79th Reserve and 221st divisions were deployed to form a second line around Arvillers and Bouchoir. In the late afternoon of 8 August the 121st and 204th divisions were ordered to Roye. Despite these moves, however, Rupprecht's headquarters also made the alarming report that owing to a shortage of artillery the planned counterstroke could not be launched before the morning of 10 August.

9 AUGUST 1918

Rawlinson's decision to retain control of his reserves on the evening of 8/9 August had a dramatic effect on the development of the battle. Rather than repeating the coordinated attacks of the first day, 9 August saw all three British corps launching separate assaults in a piecemeal fashion. Rawlinson's orders directed the Canadians towards Roye–Hattencourt–Hallu, the Australians towards Lihons and III Corps to Etinehem. Currie and Butler were given the freedom of choosing the time of attack for their respective corps, whilst Monash had the unenviable task of maintaining contact with each of his neighbours. Kavanagh had withdrawn the cavalry divisions for the night and issued orders for the 2nd Cavalry Division to support the Canadian Corps' advance on Roye, and for the 1st Cavalry Division to support the Australian advance on Chaulnes. The 3rd Cavalry Division was to be held in reserve.

The retention of 32nd Division by Fourth Army forced the Canadians to redraft their orders, using 3rd Canadian Division instead, who were still deployed around their objectives from the initial attack. Currie's plan envisaged an advance on Roye in two phases, taking the line Folies, Beaufort, Warvillers, Vrély and Rosières as the first objective and the line Andechy, Damery, Fouquescourt, Chilly and Lihons as their second objective. The 1st and 2nd Canadian divisions were to 'sideslip' to the right in order to reduce the front of the tired 3rd Canadian Division. Despite this confusion, whilst the remainder of the Canadians Corps conducted their battle procedure for the coming attack, the 4th Canadian Division recommenced their attack on Le Quesnel at 0430hrs. The attack was delivered by the 75th (Mississauga) Battalion of the 11th Canadian Brigade but was held up by stiff resistance from the 1st and 59th reserve regiments of the 1st Reserve Division. Although the village was cleared within an hour, the defenders fought tenaciously through the woods to the east and it was after midday before the objective line was taken. As a consequence of this resistance and poor communications delaying the issue of the new orders to the forward areas, H-hour was slipped, firstly from 0500 to 1100hrs for the corps as a whole, and then incrementally for each division and brigade as they struggled into position.

The DH9 was introduced in 1917. At Amiens, 27, 49, 98 and 107 squadrons of IX Brigade were equipped with this type. It had a maximum speed of 182km/ph and a service ceiling of 4,725m. It was armed with two or three .303in. machine guns and could carry up to 210kg of bombs. (IWM Q 56858)

RIGHT
Ernst Udet in front of his Fokker DVII. The DVII possessed a new, thicker wing that was able to generate much more lift than the more standard thin wings on other aircraft types. This capability was enhanced by the new 185hp BMW engines which gave the DVII a top speed of 201km/ph and a better rate of climb that any Allied aircraft. (IWM Q 63153)

BELOW RIGHT
German prisoners arriving at a POW cage at Amiens on 9 August. By the close of the second day Fourth Army had taken 387 officers and 15,516 other ranks prisoner, whilst the French First Army had captured 150 officers and 4,300 other ranks. The size of the haul after two days combat clearly demonstrated the shattered morale of the German Second Army. (IWM Q 9193)

Lüttwitz did not waste this opportunity and deployed additional reserves to reinforce his divisions already engaged with the Canadians. Having travelled throughout the night, by 0900hrs the 221st Division was beginning to occupy its new positions between Arvillers and Saulchoy, whilst the 79th Reserve Division deployed into the area between Folies and Bouchoir with a view to mounting a counterattack if possible.

The 2nd Canadian Division on the corps' left was first to move as the redeployment of its brigades was less dramatic than the other divisions. First to attack was the 6th Canadian Brigade on the left of the division. Already in position, the brigade decided to take advantage of the thin artillery barrage after arranging support from the Australians on their left. The 31st (Alberta) and 29th (Vancouver) battalions, supported by the 9th Cavalry Brigade, came under heavy machine-gun fire from front and flank as they moved towards Rosières, which was defended by the reinforced remnants of the 117th and 225th divisions. Five tanks of the 14th Tank Battalion joined the attack and worked in combination with trench mortars and ground attack aircraft to destroy the forward defensive posts. By 1330hrs the Canadians were in the town; however, it took a further three hours of heavy fighting before Rosières itself was cleared. An outpost line was then established on the Rosières–Méharicourt road, where it remained until nightfall.

On the right flank of 6th Canadian Brigade, the 22nd (French Canadian) and 25th (Nova Scotia Rifles) battalions of 5th Canadian Brigade began their advance by company between 1145 and 1300hrs. Supported by the 2nd Cavalry Brigade and 14 tanks of the 14th Tank Battalion, the Canadian infantry were soon engaged with the 46th and 58th infantry regiments of the 119th Division. In order to avoid the heavy machine-gun fire sweeping the areas of open ground, the attackers used ditches, sunken lanes and dead ground under covering fire from their Lewis guns to eliminate the German machine-gun nests one by one. By 1730hrs the brigade was digging in 450m east of Méharicourt whilst elements of the 2nd Cavalry Brigade pushed patrols out towards Fouquescourt. This area formed the western edge of the old 1916 Somme battlefield and the cavalry suffered heavy casualties as they attacked further German positions. They withdrew and joined the infantry around Méharicourt.

The assault of the 1st Canadian Division was also delayed as both the 1st and 2nd Canadian brigades were forced to move to their right by 2.3km with neither in position by 1100hrs.

The 2nd Canadian Brigade on the left moved off towards Warvillers and Vrély at 1300hrs, supported by two regiments of the 3rd Cavalry Brigade, 14 tanks of the 4th Tank Battalion and seven Whippet tanks, but without a covering barrage as the alteration in H-hour had not been passed to the artillery. The defenders were drawn from the 46th Reserve Infantry Regiment of the 119th Division, and the Canadians were soon heavily engaged with

A crashed Sopwith Camel near to Proyart on 10 August. The absence of damage to the propeller or fire damage, suggests that this aircraft failed to complete a forced landing safely. (IWM Q 3874)

their machine-gun nests. In the flat, crop-covered countryside the Canadians used short rushes by sections in combination with their Lewis gun teams to eliminate each post in turn. Particular resistance was met at Hatchet Wood, where over 300 prisoners were taken. Despite heavy casualties, by 1630hrs both the village and wood of Warvillers were captured.

The 1st Canadian Brigade began their attack on Beaufort and Rouvroy at 1315hrs supported by one regiment of the 3rd Cavalry Brigade and seven Whippet tanks. The forward elements of 'Bellmann's Regiment' were pushed back as the defensive fire of the German machine-gun posts intensified. Like their compatriots in the 2nd Canadian Brigade, the Canadians were able to utilize short forward rushes by sections to continue their advance. Having been driven out of Beaufort the German defenders fell back to positions on the high ground south of Rouvroy before they could force a temporary halt to the attack. Brigadier-General Griesbach, the brigade commander, launched his final reserve battalion in an evening attack that secured the village by 2120hrs, at which point the 1st Canadian Division halted for the night.

The 3rd Canadian Division formed the right flank of the corps attack with 8th Canadian Brigade in the lead. The brigade was already moving forwards when new orders were received at 0915hrs that two battalions, supported by seven tanks of the 5th Tank Battalion, were to take Folies as advance guard of the division. The time taken to reconnoitre, plan and deliver orders delayed the deployment and the assault of the 4th Canadian Mounted Rifles (CMR) until 1400hrs with the 5th CMR moving off at 1450hrs. Folies was secured by the 4th CMR by 1615hrs and reported little resistance; however, the advance of the 5th CMR on their right met stronger opposition from the troops of the 1st Reserve Infantry Regiment attempting to hold blocking positions on the Amiens–Roye road and from the 59th Reserve Infantry Regiment to the south of the road in the French sector. Nevertheless the advance continued by the same 'section rush' method used elsewhere and by 1700hrs Bouchoir was captured.

By the end of the day, the Canadian Corps had managed to gain only the first of its objectives and remained well short of Roye. To a great extent this was a result of the delays caused by the withholding of 32nd Division from the Canadian Corps, which added confusion amongst the Canadian divisions and brigades causing them to launch their attacks in a disjointed fashion.

Having been forced back throughout the day, Lüttwitz had been unable to launch his planned counterattack. Although the remnants of the 1st Reserve and 82nd divisions had managed to hold a line as they withdrew, they had been driven right back into the forward positions of the 221st and 79th reserve divisions and had taken severe casualties in the process. Consequently, at 1900hrs III Corps ordered their withdrawal over the coming night.

At noon on the 8th, Monash had first warned his divisional commanders to be prepared to continue the advance and ordered the 1st Australian Division to move forwards to Hamel. Although tasked to cover the inner flanks of both the Canadian and III Corps, Monash acknowledged that the main effort rested with the Canadians and drafted a plan that envisaged his corps advancing on the right whilst holding its position on the Somme until III Corps came up on the left. As this would result in an extension in the Australian front, Monash planned to insert the 1st and 2nd Australian divisions through the 5th Australian Division, with the 3rd Australian Division relieving the 4th Australian Division next to the Somme.

Corps orders were issued at 0200hrs on 9 August, stating H-Hour as not before 1000hrs that day. However, the time taken to disseminate this information to the battalions of the 1st Australian Division meant that they were unable to set out from Hamel until 0845hrs and make for their assembly area 16km distant. Despite the delay to the Canadian attack until 1100hrs it was clear that 1st Australian Division would not be in place in time. Consequently, the 6th Canadian Brigade requested that 15th Australian

British cavalry at Beaucourt on 9 August. Although the cavalry were unable to break through the German defences, they were effective in securing deep objectives for the Infantry to occupy later. (IWM Q 8198)

The 1st Australian Division advancing towards Lihons on 9 August. (IWM E(Aus)2846)

Brigade advance with them at 1100hrs in order to cover their left flank. After gaining permission from Major-General Hobbs, Brigadier-General 'Pompey' Elliott agreed and the 60th (Victoria) and 58th (Victoria) battalions were warned to advance with the Canadians at zero. However, whereas the Canadians would have artillery and tank support, the original Australian plan had dispensed with artillery owing to the allocation of tanks. The tanks, however, were still moving forwards with 1st Australian Division, which meant that Elliott's men would move without any support at all. Immediately after crossing the Amiens Defence Line they came under heavy machine-gun fire from the forward positions of the 2nd Grenadier and 26th Reserve regiments of the 109th Division and after 90m they were forced to take cover.

The 8th Australian Brigade began their advance on the left of 15th Australian Brigade at 1140hrs. A lone German field gun in Vauvillers quickly knocked out the handful of tanks that joined this attack. Trench mortars put this gun out of action and the Australians continued their attack by section rushes, supported now by RAF aircraft which repeatedly attacked any German positions they could identify. At this point the leading elements of 1st Australian Division streamed forwards towards the battle from Bayonvillers in full view of the defenders. Faced with these fresh troops and under steady pressure on their front, the troops of the 2nd Grenadier and 26th Infantry regiments began to withdraw, losing several hundred men as prisoners, including III/26th Infantry Regiment in its entirety, as they did so. Despite their lack of support, the 8th and 15th Australian brigades had taken most of the first objectives of 1st Australian Division who now took over the attack.

With Lihons as his objective, Major-General Glasgow decided to attack with the 2nd Australian Brigade leading and 3rd Australian Brigade in reserve. The 2nd Australian Brigade was to take the second objective, which lay on the eastern side of the valley between Vauvillers and Lihons. If casualties were light it was to continue its attack and take Lihons itself. If this was not possible 3rd Australian Brigade was to take over and launch an attack later in the day.

The 2nd Australian Brigade commenced its attack at 1345hrs with two battalions leading, each supported by seven tanks of the 2nd Tank Battalion

9 August 1918, order, counter-order, disorder

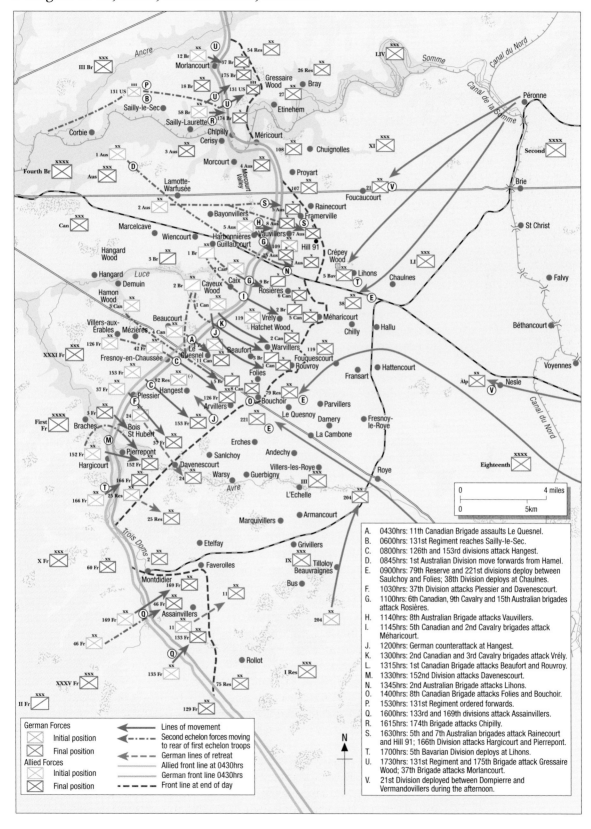

A. 0430hrs: 11th Canadian Brigade assaults Le Quesnel.
B. 0600hrs: 131st Regiment reaches Sailly-le-Sec.
C. 0800hrs: 126th and 153rd divisions attack Hangest.
D. 0845hrs: 1st Australian Division move forwards from Hamel.
E. 0900hrs: 79th Reserve and 221st divisions deploy between Saulchoy and Folies; 38th Division deploys at Chaulnes.
F. 1030hrs: 37th Division attacks Plessier and Davenescourt.
G. 1100hrs: 6th Canadian, 9th Cavalry and 15th Australian brigades attack Rosières.
H. 1140hrs: 8th Australian Brigade attacks Vauvillers.
I. 1145hrs: 5th Canadian and 2nd Cavalry brigades attack Méharicourt.
J. 1200hrs: German counterattack at Hangest.
K. 1300hrs: 2nd Canadian and 3rd Cavalry brigades attack Vrély.
L. 1315hrs: 1st Canadian Brigade attacks Beaufort and Rouvroy.
M. 1330hrs: 152nd Division attacks Davenescourt.
N. 1345hrs: 2nd Australian Brigade attacks Lihons.
O. 1400hrs: 8th Canadian Brigade attacks Folies and Bouchoir.
P. 1530hrs: 131st Regiment ordered forwards.
Q. 1600hrs: 133rd and 169th divisions attack Assainvillers.
R. 1615hrs: 174th Brigade attacks Chipilly.
S. 1630hrs: 5th and 7th Australian brigades attack Rainecourt and Hill 91; 166th Division attacks Hargicourt and Pierrepont.
T. 1700hrs: 5th Bavarian Division deploys at Lihons.
U. 1730hrs: 131st Regiment and 175th Brigade attack Gressaire Wood; 37th Brigade attacks Morlancourt.
V. 21st Division deployed between Dompierre and Vermandovillers during the afternoon.

German Forces
⊠ Initial position
⊠ Final position
Allied Forces
⊠ Initial position
⊠ Final position

⟵ Lines of movement
⟵ Second echelon forces moving to rear of first echelon troops
⟵ German lines of retreat
— Allied front line at 0430hrs
— German front line 0430hrs
--- Front line at end of day

N

and by two field guns of the 189th Brigade RFA. The ground over which they had to advance was a bare, grass-covered plain, crossed by the old trenches of the 1916 battle. In the valley, east of Vauvillers, and around Lihons, lay the artillery positions of the 109th Division and small groups of the shattered infantry regiments attempting to retire. The German gunners immediately brought the tanks under fire and five were destroyed quickly. The Australian infantry continued to advance by short section rushes, but an attempt to silence the German guns by the 189th Brigade RFA was quickly over-whelmed. Despite significant losses, the Australians used the old trench systems to provide cover for their troops to continue to work their way forwards. However, the left of 2nd Australian Brigade did not advance as quickly as the right owing to the fact that the 2nd Australian Division, which should have been on that flank, had not begun its attack. Consequently, the 7th (Victoria) Battalion was forced to form a defensive flank at 1630hrs draining the brigade's momentum.

The 2nd Australian Division had spent the day desperately attempting to speed up their preparations to overcome the delays caused by the overnight confusion. Despite the best efforts of the brigade and battalion command teams, the division was unable to commence its attack before 1630hrs. However, when it did move it immediately allowed 1st Australian Division to restart its assault on Lihons. By 1700hrs the left of the 2nd Australian Brigade had begun to work its way forwards but at this juncture significant numbers of German troops were observed moving into trenches either side of Crépey Wood on the western outskirts of Lihons. These troops were the leading elements of the 5th Bavarian Division, which was now coming into the line alongside those of the 38th Division, who deployed astride the Amiens–Chaulnes railway in the morning.

The 2nd Australian Division attacked with the 5th and 7th Australian brigades in line with 13 Mk V* tanks of the 15th Tank Battalion in support. The remnants of the 109th Division were quickly driven from Hill 91, 1,400m east of Vauvillers, but 107th Division deployed between Framerville and Proyart delivered more significant resistance. Unmolested by an attack to their front, both the 232nd Infantry Regiment of 107th Division and the 122nd Infantry Regiment under command of 108th Division were able to pour machine-gun fire into the left flank of the Australians advancing south of the Roman road. A battery of the 213th Artillery Regiment advanced onto the spur east of Rainecourt and engaged the 5th and 7th Australian brigades from their front and forced them to ground on the eastern edge of Framerville.

The presence of German reinforcements between Chaulnes and Lihons had been observed by reconnaissance aircraft and reported to Lt. Gen. Monash by 1400hrs. On learning of the Canadian halt on his right and being aware of his own troops' positions he then ordered the advance to halt on the second objective for the night.

The fighting north of the Somme followed the same confused pattern as that to the south. Having gained permission to use the American 131st Infantry Regiment, Butler issued orders at 2215hrs on the evening of the 8th to continue the attack the next day. Following its losses over three days of fighting, the 18th Division was to be withdrawn. On the right, the 58th Division was to attack towards the north-east and east in order to take Gressaire Wood and the Chipilly Spur, whilst on the left the 12th Division was to complete the capture of Morlancourt and advance to the Amiens Outer Defence Line. Owing to the distance the 131st Infantry Regiment needed to cover to reach their attack

positions, it was impossible to launch the attack at dawn and a postponement to the afternoon was ordered at 0220hrs on 9 August.

The 58th Division was to attack with 174th Brigade on the right with Chipilly as the objective, 131st Regiment in the centre and 175th Brigade on the left both attacking Gressaire Wood. The 173rd Brigade was to cover the right flank of the 131st Regiment as it moved forwards. At 1615hrs the 6th Londons, only 96 men strong, moved on Chipilly and were immediately assailed by heavy machine-gun fire from both flanks bringing them to a halt. The commanding officer of the 2/10th Londons moved his unit forwards in support and, by using dead ground and short section rushes, was able to advance before he too was held up by machine-gun nests north of Chipilly. Observing this action from south of the Somme was Brigadier-General Mackay of the 1st Australian Brigade. He ordered a patrol to be sent across the river, led by CQMS Hayes and Sgt. Andrews who had both been through Chipilly that morning. Taking four other men, Hayes and Andrews crossed the river at 1800hrs and, disregarding the advice of a company commander of the 2/10th Londons, pushed onwards, identifying several machine-gun posts on the Chipilly Spur as they went. Taking advantage of a smoke barrage fired in support of the main attack to the north, the Australians continued to move round to the flank of these posts and began to attack the German posts on the rear of the spur. Andrews then set up a German machine gun to engage the German troops who were beginning to withdraw back over the river. The Londons moved round to assist and, by 2000hrs, 200 prisoners had been taken.

To the north the attack of the American 131st Regiment did not go smoothly because of poor staff work by III Corps. The Americans reached their assembly positions on the Bray–Corbie road above Sailly-Le-Sec at 0600hrs on the 9th but received no hot food or drink after an overnight approach march of over 30km. At 1300hrs, they received a warning order detailing them to take part in the attack on Gressaire Wood that evening.

Australian infantry attacking at Verugier in September 1918. Although this image was taken approximately one month after Amiens, it gives an evocative illustration of the infantry in open warfare in late 1918. (IWM E(Aus) 3260)

Exhausted Australian troops resting in an old trench in front of Crépey Wood. In front of the two soldiers standing in the centre is a rifle fitted with a cup discharger for a rifle grenade. (IWM E(Aus) 2870)

Despite having been stationary for nine and a half hours only 5km from their jump-off positions, the regiment was further warned at 1530hrs that the attack would be launched 90 minutes later. The attack was further delayed until 1730hrs, but it still left only two hours to cover the ground and issue orders. In the confusion the operations officer rounded up the regiment and got it moving forwards at a rapid pace in order not to miss the artillery barrage meant to cover their assault. Meanwhile the commander, Colonel Sanborne, moved forwards to reconnoitre in less than ideal circumstances. Little more could be done than mark out the jump-off line on the forward edge of Malard Wood.

Sanborne planned to attack with 2/131st left, 1/131st right and 3/131st in reserve, with the troops deploying straight into their attacking formations from the line of march. Sanborne briefed his battalion commanders as best he could, who in turn attempted to disseminate the plan to their men. The attack moved off on time but was lashed with machine-gun fire from both Gressaire Wood to the front and the Chipilly Spur on the flank. After two hours' hard fighting the American troops had covered the distance to Gressaire Wood and remained engaged in a heavy firefight. As they continued to push the defenders from the 27th Division back, the Württemburgers, fearing envelopment from the south, began to withdraw their line to the Méault–Etinehem road. At 2120hrs the fighting in Gressaire Wood died down and the Americans prepared to hold their gains during the coming night.

On the left flank of III Corps, 37th Brigade of 12th Division met heavy opposition as it attempted to reach its objectives around Morlancourt. A tank detailed to support the attack arrived 15 minutes early and was promptly destroyed by a field gun. With the defenders of the 54th Reserve Division now alerted, the infantry attacked into heavy machine-gun and trench mortar fire. They quickly crossed no man's land and began to work parties round to the rear of the village. Once this had been achieved the resistance slackened and the objectives for the day had been taken.

The French First Army continued its advance on Roye on 9 August by extending its attack to the south on either side of Montdidier. X Corps crossed the Avre at Neuville and swung round to the south-east on the right flank of the XXXI Corps. Later, XXXV Corps broke into the German defences at Assainvillers in order to drive directly to Roye from the south-west.

XXXI Corps relieved the 42nd Division with the 126th Division on the left, keeping the 153rd Division in the centre and the 37th Division on the right. The attack of the 126th Division began at 0800hrs but was poorly coordinated between artillery and infantry. Hangest was captured by 1020hrs but the attack was held up by machine-gun fire from 1st Reserve Division and elements of 82nd Reserve Division. At 1300hrs a German counterattack imposed a further delay and it was not until 1600hrs that the advance was resumed. By 1745hrs the 126th Division came to rest in Arvillers.

The 153rd Division also moved off at 0800hrs, supported by the light tank battalions and artillery. Although Hangest was captured in conjunction with the 126th Division, the tired troops were prevented from advancing beyond the village by machine-gun fire from the 82nd Reserve Division. At midday a counterattack was launched by two battalions of the 221st Division who drove the French back a short distance before being halted by artillery fire. At this point in the battle, the tanks were withdrawn for maintenance. This exhausted the 153rd Division and a subsequent attempt to advance at 1800hrs only made 200m.

The 37th Division renewed its attack at 1030hrs but faced similar difficulties to the divisions to the north. The right flank of the German 24th Division held strong positions on the Hangest–Davenescourt ridge, which halted 37th Division in its tracks. It took until 1730hrs to organize artillery support and when the attack was resumed only a limited advance on the left could be made. The division came to rest having moved forwards only 3km in the day.

The 3rd Division completed IX Corps' tasks by occupying the Bois St Hubert after the German 179th Infantry Regiment withdrew. The 152nd Division crossed the Avre at Braches at 1130hrs, and by 1330hrs had commenced its advance east of the Bois St Hubert as the 139th Infantry Regiment struggled to hold the centre of the 24th Division sector. By nightfall the 152nd Division was in front of Davenescourt on the flank of the 37th Division. Having completed their task, IX Corps was withdrawn to the reserves of the First Army.

An Australian 4.5in. howitzer battery in action on 8 August. Like the 60-pdr, the 4.5 was brought into service in 1904 as a result of experience in the Boer War. By 1918 it equipped the heavy batteries of the divisional artillery brigades and fired a 16kg shell 6,675m. (IWM E(Aus) 2854)

Troops of the 58th Division cleaning weapons and receiving a brief on the Chipilly Spur. The 58th Division was originally raised from Territorial Army units in London and had been involved heavily engaged in the defensive battles of 1918, particularly at Villers-Bretonneux. The attack of 27th (Württemburg) Division on 6 August struck the left flank of the 58th and in effect started the battle two days earlier than the Dominion troops south of the Somme. (IWM Q 9190)

The slow progress of the First Army during the morning caused Foch great concern. On two occasions he urged Debeney to drive his troops towards Roye, '… without losing a minute …', and forbidding the withdrawal of divisions from the front line. The latter demand was almost impossible to meet as the lack of space available to Debeney gave him little option but to withdraw the units on the Avre as XXXI Corps moved past them.

The 166th Division attacked in the centre of X Corps' sector at 1630hrs, crossing the Trois Doms stream at Hargicourt and Pierrepont. Determined resistance by the 133rd Infantry Regiment on the left flank of 24th Division coupled with the difficulty in crossing the marshes in the valley limited the penetration to the Amiens–Montdidier road. On the right flank of X Corps, 60th Division held their lines in front of Montdidier, between the attacks to their north and south.

The development of the First Army's attack south of Montdidier did not achieve Debeney's aim as XXXV Corps was unable to clear a route for II Cavalry Corps. Debeney postponed the attack until 1600hrs following the delay in capturing Hangest. Jacquot's plan was for the 169th Division to secure a breach in the German line through which the 46th Division would move to take over the attack. The 133rd Division was to cover the right flank of the First Army. The German defences in this sector were more developed than farther north, built on mutually supporting strongpoints with excellent fields of observation and fire, and were occupied by the 2nd and 11th divisions of Oetinger's IX Corps. In order to achieve and maintain surprise, no bombardment was to be fired prior to H-Hour and a rapid advance was demanded of the French infantry.

At 1600hrs the 169th Division attacked behind a heavy artillery bombardment and rolling barrage. Despite strong opposition from the 11th Division, the French drove forwards and by 1805hrs had captured Assainvillers by envelopment from the west and north-west, taking 250 prisoners. The 133rd Division launched its assault at the same time, with a

LEFT
The wreckage of a DFW south of Vermandovillers on 10 August. Although the DFW had been used by the Schlastas in 1917, by 1918 it had become the workhorse of the FA(A) units. Although the unit of this aircraft is unknown, it is possible that it was that flown by *Leutnants der Reserve* Diebler and Jensen of FA 241(A), who were both killed when shot down in this area on 8 August. (IWM E(Aus) 2875)

BELOW LEFT
Bréguet 14 B2 bomber. The Br 14 was the workhorse of the French bomber squadrons in 1918. It had a maximum speed of 177km/ph and a service ceiling of 5,800m. It could carry 300kg of bombs. (IWM Q 67910)

strong reserve in order to meet the expected counterattack from the right flank. By 1800hrs the division was on its final objective astride the Roye–Rollot road where it consolidated a defensive line facing north-east.

Unfortunately, the opportunity to exploit the break-in was missed, as the 46th Division was unable to follow up the 169th Division and attack Faverolles. Arriving in XXXV Corps only 48 hours earlier the 46th Division was unable to establish effective liaison either with the corps HQ or other divisional HQ staffs. This situation was exacerbated by the lack of cover to the rear of the 169th Division, the delay of H-Hour and their unfamiliarity with the sector. Consequently, the leading elements were too far behind the 169th Division and were slow in reading the battle. By the time night fell, and having advanced with difficulty, they remained no farther forwards than the Montdidier–Assainvillers road.

Battle of the bridges

German reinforcement of their air units continued on 9 August with the elite JG II and JG III transferring to the Eighteenth Army from the Ninth Army in Champagne and Seventh Army on the Chemin de Dames respectively. With

The bridge over the Somme Canal at Béthancourt. The objective of sustained RAF attacks between 8 and 10 August, the bridge escaped serious damage and continues to carry traffic over the canal to this day. (Author's collection)

the Somme bridges remaining the focus of the air battle, IX Brigade RAF continued the assault with raids overnight, and resumed the daylight attack at first light. In view of the difficulties caused by the defending German aircraft on 8 August, the escorting fighters did not carry bombs but were now tasked solely with the protection of the bombers. Between 0500 and 0515hrs, 27 and 49 squadrons set off to attack the bridges at Falvy, Béthancourt and Voyennes at low level. German fighters were encountered but no aircraft were lost. Others were not so lucky. Farther north, 107 Squadron was decimated whilst attacking the bridge at Brie with three formations of five DH9s, escorted by Sopwith Camels of 54 Squadron. The first two formations bombed with little success under increasing levels of attack. The third formation met the now fully alert fliers of JG I and Jasta 27, losing three DH9s and two Camels in the ensuing dogfight.

After further ineffective raids on other bridges in the morning, RAF tactics were changed for the attacks in the afternoon. All available bombers from IX Brigade were now to attack their objectives simultaneously at 1700hrs, with a close escort provided by IX Brigade fighters and a high escort provided by I Brigade aircraft brought down from the north for the mission. All together 30 bombers escorted by 124 fighters launched the attacks on the bridges at Eclusier, Brie, Béthancourt and Falvy. Although no aircraft were lost, coordination between the escorts and bombers was poor. The raid against Falvy was turned back and no hits were recorded on any of the target bridges.

Improvements in the weather saw the Division Aérienne come into the battle during the day. Whilst the *groupes de combat* protected the reconnaissance and artillery observation aircraft of the First Army, the *groupes de bombardement* attacked the railheads at Roye, Fresnoy-le-Roye, Fransart and Hombleux, and troop concentration areas at Tilloloy, Beuvraignes and Bus.

Command decisions

Disappointed at the progress made during the day, Haig's staff simply restated the same objectives for 10 August. By way of reinforcement, the 32nd Division was finally released to the Canadian Corps. Monash meanwhile was developing new plans to deal with the tactical problem posed by the

10 August 1918, Hutier withdraws

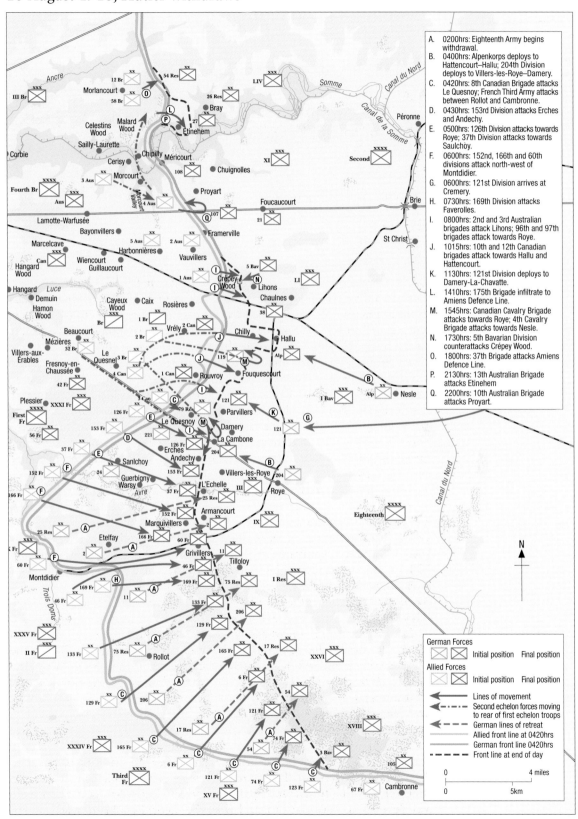

A. 0200hrs: Eighteenth Army begins withdrawal.

B. 0400hrs: Alpenkorps deploys to Hattencourt–Hallu; 204th Division deploys to Villers-les-Roye–Damery.

C. 0420hrs: 8th Canadian Brigade attacks Le Quesnoy; French Third Army attacks between Rollot and Cambronne.

D. 0430hrs: 153rd Division attacks Erches and Andechy.

E. 0500hrs: 126th Division attacks towards Roye; 37th Division attacks towards Saulchòy.

F. 0600hrs: 152nd, 166th and 60th divisions attack north-west of Montdidier.

G. 0600hrs: 121st Division arrives at Cremery.

H. 0730hrs: 169th Division attacks Faverolles.

I. 0800hrs: 2nd and 3rd Australian brigades attack Lihons; 96th and 97th brigades attack towards Roye.

J. 1015hrs: 10th and 12th Canadian brigades attack towards Hallu and Hattencourt.

K. 1130hrs: 121st Division deploys to Damery-La-Chavatte.

L. 1410hrs: 175th Brigade infiltrate to Amiens Defence Line.

M. 1545hrs: Canadian Cavalry Brigade attacks towards Roye; 4th Cavalry Brigade attacks towards Nesle.

N. 1730hrs: 5th Bavarian Division counterattacks Crépey Wood.

O. 1800hrs: 37th Brigade attacks Amiens Defence Line.

P. 2130hrs: 13th Australian Brigade attacks Etinehem

Q. 2200hrs: 10th Australian Brigade attacks Proyart.

German Forces

| | | Initial position | Final position |

Allied Forces

| | | Initial position | Final position |

⟵ Lines of movement

⟵ Second echelon forces moving to rear of first echelon troops

⟵ German lines of retreat

 Allied front line at 0420hrs

 German front line at 0420hrs

 Front line at end of day

0 ——— 4 miles

0 ——— 5km

N

An Australian OP within 200m of the German line at Lihons. The fighting conditions of 1918 meant that significant gaps existed between defended localities. In order to maintain an effective defence, each gap needed to be kept under constant surveillance to detect any approaching enemy and to call down protective artillery, trench mortar or machine-gun fire. (IWM E(Aus) 2872)

meandering course of the Somme and the projecting spurs it created. In order to put these into action he asked for the northern boundary of his corps to be extended across the Somme to the Corbie–Bray road. This was granted. To the south, Général Fayolle decided that the time had come to commit the Third Army to the battle and ordered Humbert to attack.

Within Heeresgruppe Rupprecht, both Marwitz and Hutier raised concerns over the results of the day's fighting. At 1620hrs, Marwitz reported that his troops were exhausted and requested permission to withdraw behind the Somme overnight. Rupprecht's chief of staff, Kuhl, refused due to the difficulties such a manoeuvre would cause Eighteenth Army to the south, and promised Marwitz fresh troops. At 2200hrs, however, following the French attack south of Montdidier, Kuhl was informed by Hutier that Eighteenth Army would be forced to withdraw as III Corps' positions were now untenable, and it was agreed to withdraw the right wing of his army onto a line between l'Echelle–Conchy–Ricquebourg in the coming night. On arrival at this line the right wing of the Eighteenth Army would be reinforced by I Bavarian Corps, consisting of the Alpenkorps, 121st and 204th divisions, under General Ritter von Endres, which was now concentrating in the Roye area and which had been placed at Hutier's disposal.

10 AUGUST 1918

The battle on the Australian Corps' front developed into two separate engagements; the continuing struggle for Lihons and Monash's fresh attempt to capture the Etinehem and Méricourt spurs to secure his left flank along the Somme.

Monash issued orders on the evening of 9 August that 1st Australian Division would renew the attack towards Lihons at 0800hrs the next day following confirmation of Currie's intentions. Major-General Glasgow's plan was to attack with 2nd Australian Brigade on the right, 3rd Australian Brigade on the left and 1st Australian Brigade in support. No tanks were allocated to support the attack, which was to be delivered behind a barrage commencing at 0745hrs. The battle procedure of the attacking troops was not straightforward as the leading battalions of 3rd Australian Brigade had to relieve the troops of 2nd Australian Brigade on the left of the divisional front, to enable 2nd Australian Brigade to slip to the right to occupy their assault positions. This was not achieved until 0745hrs and was spotted by a German reconnaissance aircraft, which alerted the defenders. Uncertainty over the forward Australian positions stripped the barrage of any utility as it was subsequently fired at a 'safe' distance, 650m in front of the assumed jump-off line and therefore beyond the foremost positions of the 19th, 21st and 7th Bavarian infantry regiments.

As the Australians moved off a furious curtain of fire met them and they suffered severe casualties amongst the company officers. The attack swung towards the south as the battalions struggled to hold direction. The 3rd Australian Brigade surrounded Crépey Wood and organized a line on its eastern edge. To the south, 2nd Australian Brigade worked methodically forwards and captured Factory Wood despite sustaining heavy casualties. However, it was subsequently halted by fire from German posts holding out in Crépey Wood. These were suppressed by fire from a trench mortar battery and cleared by the reserve battalions of the 3rd Australian Brigade. Tired by their previous exertions and deprived of their officers, the troops of the 1st Australian Division hesitated and the attack stalled.

The 5th Bavarian Division was not minded to let them rest, however, and at 1730hrs a German bombardment fell on Crépey Wood, announcing the impending arrival of a counterattack. II/19th and III/21st Bavarian infantry regiments hurled themselves at the wood from three sides and entered it at several points. However, the Australians held firm and drove the attack back, inflicting 250 casualties on III/21st Bavarian Infantry Regiment. The fighting in front of Lihons died down for the evening whilst Monash organized its resumption at 0400hrs the next day.

North of the Somme, Major-General MacLagan's 4th Australian Division was ordered to take over the line up to the Bray–Corbie road by 0800hrs.

German wounded at a dressing station in Chipilly on 10 August. Advanced dressing stations (ADS) were formed by Field Ambulance personnel and were deployed as far forward as possible. At least one ADS was established per Division with more being used if suitable accommodation and evacuation routes were available. Each required shelter for at least 100 casualties who would be 'triaged' (sorted and prioritized) according to clinical need, prior to evacuation by motor ambulance. (IWM Q 6943)

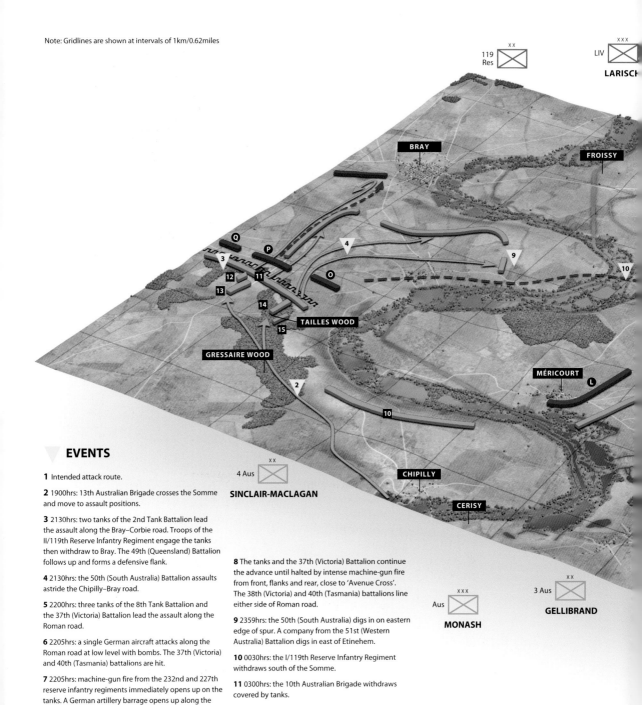

Note: Gridlines are shown at intervals of 1km/0.62miles

119 Res XX

LIV XXX
LARISCH

BRAY

FROISSY

Q

P

3

12

11

O

4

9

10

13

14

TAILLES WOOD

15

GRESSAIRE WOOD

MÉRICOURT

L

2

10

EVENTS

1 Intended attack route.

2 1900hrs: 13th Australian Brigade crosses the Somme and move to assault positions.

3 2130hrs: two tanks of the 2nd Tank Battalion lead the assault along the Bray–Corbie road. Troops of the II/119th Reserve Infantry Regiment engage the tanks then withdraw to Bray. The 49th (Queensland) Battalion follows up and forms a defensive flank.

4 2130hrs: the 50th (South Australia) Battalion assaults astride the Chipilly–Bray road.

5 2200hrs: three tanks of the 8th Tank Battalion and the 37th (Victoria) Battalion lead the assault along the Roman road.

6 2205hrs: a single German aircraft attacks along the Roman road at low level with bombs. The 37th (Victoria) and 40th (Tasmania) battalions are hit.

7 2205hrs: machine-gun fire from the 232nd and 227th reserve infantry regiments immediately opens up on the tanks. A German artillery barrage opens up along the Roman road.

8 The tanks and the 37th (Victoria) Battalion continue the advance until halted by intense machine-gun fire from front, flanks and rear, close to 'Avenue Cross'. The 38th (Victoria) and 40th (Tasmania) battalions line either side of Roman road.

9 2359hrs: the 50th (South Australia) digs in on eastern edge of spur. A company from the 51st (Western Australia) Battalion digs in east of Etinehem.

10 0030hrs: the I/119th Reserve Infantry Regiment withdraws south of the Somme.

11 0300hrs: the 10th Australian Brigade withdraws covered by tanks.

12 0330hrs: the tanks withdraw.

4 Aus XX
SINCLAIR-MACLAGAN

CHIPILLY

CERISY

Aus XXX
MONASH

3 Aus XX
GELLIBRAND

ATTACK OF 10TH AND 13TH AUSTRALIAN BRIGADES AT PROYART AND ETINEHEM: 10 AUGUST

Monash conceived a complex manoeuvre to eliminate the German defences between Proyart and Etinehem. To the south, the 10th Australian Brigade was to advance to 'Avenue Cross' before swinging north to the Somme via Chuignolles to form a cordon around the forward troops of the 108th Division. These were to be cleared by a subsequent attack by the 9th and 11th Australian brigades. North of the Somme, the 13th Australian Brigade was to envelop Etinehem to the north and east.

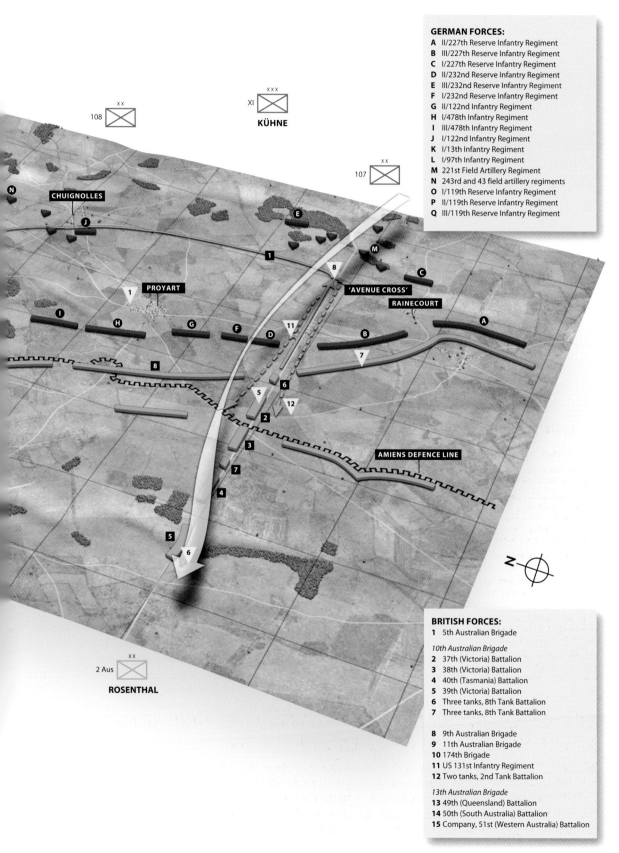

GERMAN FORCES:
A II/227th Reserve Infantry Regiment
B III/227th Reserve Infantry Regiment
C I/227th Reserve Infantry Regiment
D II/232nd Reserve Infantry Regiment
E III/232nd Reserve Infantry Regiment
F I/232nd Reserve Infantry Regiment
G II/122nd Infantry Regiment
H I/478th Infantry Regiment
I III/478th Infantry Regiment
J I/122nd Infantry Regiment
K I/13th Infantry Regiment
L I/97th Infantry Regiment
M 221st Field Artillery Regiment
N 243rd and 43 field artillery regiments
O I/119th Reserve Infantry Regiment
P II/119th Reserve Infantry Regiment
Q III/119th Reserve Infantry Regiment

108 XX

XI XXX
KÜHNE

107 XX

CHUIGNOLLES

PROYART

'AVENUE CROSS'
RAINECOURT

AMIENS DEFENCE LINE

2 Aus XX
ROSENTHAL

N Z

BRITISH FORCES:
1 5th Australian Brigade

10th Australian Brigade
2 37th (Victoria) Battalion
3 38th (Victoria) Battalion
4 40th (Tasmania) Battalion
5 39th (Victoria) Battalion
6 Three tanks, 8th Tank Battalion
7 Three tanks, 8th Tank Battalion

8 9th Australian Brigade
9 11th Australian Brigade
10 174th Brigade
11 US 131st Infantry Regiment
12 Two tanks, 2nd Tank Battalion

13th Australian Brigade
13 49th (Queensland) Battalion
14 50th (South Australia) Battalion
15 Company, 51st (Western Australia) Battalion

Monash revealed his plan to advance along the river at a conference held at 1130hrs attended by MacLagan, Brigadier-General Herring of 13th Australian Brigade, Major-General Gellibrand of 3rd Australian Division and Brigadier-General McNicholl of 10th Australian Brigade. In order to overcome the tactical problem posed by the north–south reaches of the Somme and the spurs of high ground in between them, Monash proposed to pierce the German line on the Bray–Corbie road in the north and on the Roman road in the south before swinging both attacks inwards to meet on the river at the southern end of the Etinehem Spur. The area thus isolated would then be cleared by troops on the inner flanks of 10th and 13th Australian brigades. The attack was to be launched at night and would use a small number of tanks to frighten the unsighted defenders with their noise.

The plan was ambitious and did not meet with universal approval, particularly amongst the regimental officers who would have to carry it out. The attack was due to be launched at 2130hrs; however, owing to the open nature of the ground south of the Somme, McNicholl issued orders to delay until 2200hrs in order to complete his move forwards under cover of darkness. The four battalions of 10th Australian Brigade advanced in column, led by three tanks from 8th Tank Battalion. The head of the column moved anxiously into the German lines in silence apart from the noise of the tanks. As the scouts searched for the point at which the attack would swing to the north, a German aircraft swept in at low altitude from the east dropping bombs all along the column. The defending troops of the 232nd Infantry Regiment then opened up a tremendous barrage of machine-gun fire. The column advanced slowly until it reached 'Avenue Cross' where it stopped dead in its tracks. The Australian infantry dashed for cover as best they could on either side of the road whilst armour-piercing bullets began to cause casualties to the tank crews. In the confusion it was decided to halt the attack as the Australians moved into the relative safety of the fields. The troops at the rear of the column had not escaped either as they had been raked with high explosive and gas shells from the German artillery. With the whole attack now in chaos, the brigade was ordered to withdraw under cover of the tanks, which it did by 0330hrs.

The attack of 13th Australian Brigade north of the Somme was more successful. The brigade advanced on separate routes with 49th (Queensland) Battalion to the north providing a flank guard to 50th (South Australia) Battalion, which was to advance to the east before swinging south onto the Etinehem Spur. The 49th (Queensland) Battalion was assisted by two tanks of the 2nd Tank Battalion whose fire caused much panic amongst the defenders of the 119th Infantry Regiment as Monash had hoped. This assisted 50th (South Australia) Battalion as serious resistance on their front ceased. However, owing to navigation difficulties in the dark, the whole of the Etinehem Spur was not occupied. The commander of I/119th Reserve Infantry Regiment in Etinehem realized the precarious nature of his position and withdrew his men across the Somme without further interference.

Currie's plan for 10 August was for the 32nd Division and 4th Canadian Division to pass through the 1st, 2nd and 3rd Canadian divisions and drive forwards to the line of the Roye–Chaulnes railway, with H-Hour at 0800hrs.

Prior to the main attack, at 0420hrs 8th Canadian Brigade launched an attack to complete their mission of the previous day and captured Le Quesnoy. The brigade, supported by four tanks of the 5th Tank Battalion, assaulted into heavy defensive fire from the 79th Reserve Division, which had relieved the 1st Reserve Division overnight. The tanks were all destroyed but by 0630hrs the 2nd CMR had fought its way through to the eastern side of the village and consolidated their line in the old 1916 trenches. At 0930hrs they were joined by the 1st CMR who extended the line to the north and awaited the arrival of the 32nd Division.

The 32nd Division moved forwards from its assembly area during the night and the 96th and 97th brigades crossed the start line on time, supported by 20 tanks of the 4th and 5th tank battalions. The earlier attack of 8th Canadian Brigade eased the initial advance. However, as the British pushed past Le Quesnoy and deeper into the old trench system they came under increasingly heavy machine-gun fire. Furthermore, they were not supported on either flank, as neither the French nor the 4th Canadian Division had been able to assault on time. On the right, the 96th Brigade came under fire from Parvillers and Square Wood and soon had four tanks hit by anti-tank guns. The brigade forced its way into Square Wood, but an immediate counterattack drove it back to the western edge where it clung on at 1330hrs. At 1400hrs, four more tanks arrived and supported another attack, which again captured the wood. However, the gain could not be held as yet another counterattack drove them back to the western edge where they held a line running north through Quarry Wood.

The 97th Brigade on the left also had an easy opening to their attack, but like their comrades to the south they were rapidly halted by the German defences at Parvillers and Fouquescourt. Most of the tanks were put out of action, and by 1100hrs the attack was stalled in the old British 'front line'. Although unclear as to the exact locations of his forward troops, at 1500hrs Major-General Lambert knew enough about the stiffening resistance to halt any further assault, and advised Currie that any future attack should only be launched with a planned artillery preparation. Despite these difficulties, however, 32nd Division had fought 79th Reserve Division to a standstill with the result that 221st Division, to the south of the Amiens–Roye road, was ordered to deploy its reserve regiment north from Andechy to Damery.

A Mk. V 'female' tank that ditched whilst clearing undergrowth despite being fitted with 'spuds' on each track to give better traction. The louvre panel to the rear of the sponson was part of a cooling system that attempted to improve the conditions for the crew inside. (IWM Q 6944)

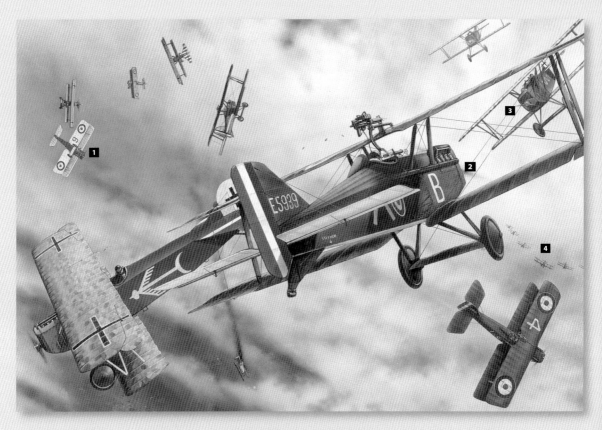

DOGFIGHT BETWEEN 32 SQUADRON RAF AND JASTA 15 (pp. 80–81)

The air operations in support of the ground battle reached their zenith of intensity on 10 August. By this time the RAF effort was shifting back towards the original intention of interdicting the German lines of communications by attacking the key railway centres through which any reinforcements would need to transit. Twelve DH9s from 27 and 49 squadrons were tasked with bombing Péronne railway station escorted by SE5as of 32 Squadron and Bristol Fighters of 62 Squadron. As they approached the target from the south-west they were attacked by 15 Fokker DVIIs from Jasta 15 led by the ace commander of JG II, Rudolf Berthold.

In order to maintain the advantage given by a higher position both attackers and defenders normally split their force with one element placed above the other to act as 'top cover'. Once under attack a defender would attempt to execute a climbing turn towards the attack to bring his own guns to bear, prevent the attacker form getting on his tail and to get above the attacker. As a consequence each combat soon degenerated into a rolling maul of aircraft climbing and turning in search of a killing shot.

Flying with 32 Squadron was Second Lieutenant J. O. Donaldson of the USAS on attachment to the RAF. Donaldson was flying as top cover as 'B5' in SE5a E5939 when:

[He] observed 9 Fokker biplanes, at 13000ft over Péronne, at 1130hrs dive on 3 SE5a **(1)**. Pilot coming to their assistance, fired 150 rounds into first EA [enemy aircraft] at close range, EA turned over on its back, and went down in a flat spin, and was observed to spin, out of control about 10000ft.

Four Fokker biplanes dived on Pilot **(2)**, who made a climbing turn, firing 50 rounds into second EA without results **(3)**. Pilot did half roll and dived again, two EA continued to follow, pilot then made another climbing turn, firing 50 rounds into EA without result. Pilot turned and dived under some Bristol Fighters **(4)**.

Combat report, Second Lieutenant J. O. Donaldson, 10 August 1918

A passing patrol from the elite 56 Squadron joined in the mêlée to stack the odds against Jasta 15, however, the powerful DVIIs were faster and more agile than their opponents and exacted a severe toll from the RAF as one DH9 and four fighters were shot down for the loss of only one German aircraft. Unfortunately for JG II the loss was Berthold who was seriously injured after having his aircraft shot out of control.

With no one able to confirm Donaldson's victim's crashing he was only credited with a 'shot down out of control' rather than a kill. Donaldson's luck ran out three weeks later on 1 September at Cambrai where he became the 11th victim of Leutnant Theo Quandt of Jasta 36 and was taken prisoner.

The 4th Canadian Division was unable to meet the 0800hrs H-Hour set by Currie as delays in issuing orders prevented the supporting tanks arriving before 1015hrs. The 10th Canadian Brigade on the right met little resistance until they reached the 1916 defences and immediately came under German artillery fire. Under cover of a strong rolling barrage, the Canadians worked methodically through the trenches and by 1400hrs were established on the western edge of Fouquescourt. The 12th Canadian Brigade on the left also made rapid progress and by 1330hrs was in possession of Chilly and Maucourt.

The second stage of the advance was more difficult as the attackers moved deeper into the trench systems around Fouquescourt and Hallu. The 10th Canadian Brigade took until 1800hrs to take a firm hold on Fouquescourt. In doing so they cleared the way for a further advance to the railway which they reached at 2045hrs. The right flank of the 12th Canadian Brigade took Hallu by 1400hrs despite the lack of support on either flank. On the left, however, flanking fire from defenders around Lihons pinned the 38th Canadian Battalion down on the Chilly–Lihons road.

As news of the day's advances came through, Kavanagh decided that the time was ripe to drive his cavalry through to the deeper objectives. At 1425hrs he issued orders for 3rd Cavalry Division to take the heights north of Roye and for 2nd Cavalry Division to occupy Nesle. The Canadian Cavalry Brigade advanced through Bouchoir at 1530hrs but having passed through 32nd Division's forward posts came under heavy fire from the 41st Infantry Regiment in Damery. Their attack swung to the right and crossed the Amiens–Roye road before seizing Andechy. This was handed over to the French who moved forwards quickly but further attempts to advance were repulsed with severe losses. To the north, the 4th Cavalry Brigade suffered a similar fate in front of Fouquescourt. Seven Whippet tanks of the 6th Tank Battalion came to grief between Rouvroy and Parvillers, whilst 16 Whippets of 3rd Tank Battalion never got into action.

The major development on the French Front was the entry of Humbert's Third Army into the battle with the XXXIV and XV corps pivoting on their right to follow the Eighteenth Army as it withdrew. In the First Army, Debeney's objectives for his Corps Commanders were the same as those he had given to them for the previous day: XXXI Corps and X Corps were to push south-east towards Roye, and link up with the XXXV Corps advancing from the south-west.

With a view to maintaining surprise and rapidity of movement, Humbert chose to open his artillery bombardment at the same time as the infantry attack was launched. At 0420hrs the six divisions of XXXIV and XV corps attacked the rearguards of the I Reserve, XXVI and XVIII corps on the left of Hutier's Army, which had commenced its withdrawal earlier in the night. Pivoting on 67th Division in XV Corps, the Third Army advanced 10km on the left as it came in line with the right flank of the XXXV Corps of the First Army, at which point it ran into the new German defensive line.

On the First Army front, XXXI Corps recommenced its attack at 0430hrs with 153rd Division in the centre, and at 0500hrs with 126th Division on the left and 37th Division on the right. The corps sector saw the stiffest resistance put up by the Germans, as the 221st Division of Lüttwitz' III Corps fought desperately to secure the right flank of the Eighteenth Army as the centre and left withdrew. The 153rd Division captured Erches by envelopment at 0945hrs and at 1135hrs gave orders to advance to Andechy and Villers-les-Roye. Andechy was taken in conjunction with the Canadian

An FE2b night bomber prepares to depart for a mission. 58, 83 and 101 squadrons were equipped with this type which they used to launch the night attacks against the Somme bridges. (IWM Q 65530)

Cavalry Brigade; however, the subsequent advance on Villers-les-Roye was postponed once it became clear that 'Z' Wood was not to be attacked that day by the 126th Division. The 126th Division advanced methodically until 1500hrs when it was halted by machine-gun fire from 'Z' Wood. Plans to assault the wood were postponed until the following day once it became clear that the Canadian Corps to the north had halted west of Damery. The 37th Division captured Saulchoy before swinging slightly to the right to maintain liaison with 152nd Division in X Corps. The division seized Guerbigny, Warsy and Marquivillers as it advanced, before the 25th Division halted it in front of Armancourt and L'Echelle.

The attack of Debeney's southern wing lacked a sense of urgency throughout the day as the divisional commanders misread the German withdrawal, despite orders from Général Jacquot to speed up. XXXV Corps' assault eventually began at 0730hrs when the 169th Division overran a small rearguard to complete the seizure of Faverolles. The 46th Division then advanced cautiously along the Montdidier–Roye road until it reached Tilloloy where contact was re-established with the Germans in the old 1916 defences. Having failed to breach the German lines, any opportunity to employ II Cavalry Corps receded dramatically. Less some squadrons left to the rear of XXXV Corps, the remainder of the cavalry withdrew to the valleys of the Avre and Trois Doms.

In X Corps, 60th Division spent the night regrouping whilst Oetinger's 25th and 2nd divisions used rifle and machine-gun fire to screen their withdrawal effectively. It was not until 1000hrs that the French occupied Montdidier. The advance continued slowly through Etelfay before halting at Grivillers under artillery and machine-gun fire as the new defence line was reached. Fighting was light throughout the day with only 13 prisoners taken and 30 casualties sustained. The 152nd Division swept up the Avre Valley until nightfall, brushing aside any rearguards until heavy artillery and machine-gun fire announced it had reached the new resistance line at Armancourt.

The air battle maintained its intensity during 10 August, which was marked by the loss of two of Germany's finest fighter pilots and a switch of strategy by the RAF. Overnight raids against the Somme bridges were continued but little damage was caused. The RAF returned to its initial objectives and redirected some of its aircraft to attack the railway junctions through which the German reinforcements were travelling.

The Division Aérienne shifted its efforts to the east as II Brigade was ordered to support the entrance of the Third Army into the battle, with the *groupes de bombardement* being placed at one hour's notice to move to engage targets between Roye and Boulogne-la-Grasse. German convoys were repeatedly attacked along the roads around Roye, although few aerial combats were fought. Large raids were launched against Lassigny by Escadre 12 and Escadre 13 in the evening, dropping over 20 tonnes of bombs.

The shock of battle resonated into the HQ of the Second Army on 10 August when Klewitz replaced Tschischwitz as army chief of staff. Noting the continued piecemeal delivery of the Allied attacks, Klewitz telephoned Kuhl at Heersgruppe Rupprecht, informing him that the Second Army's ability to hold its ground was improving and that the German line should remain west of the Somme in order to secure the right flank of Eighteenth Army. Kuhl agreed, however, he recommended that OHL should consider a future surprise withdrawal behind the Somme once the Franco-British assault ended, in order to ease the strain on his tired Armies. Unfortunately, OHL made no firm decision on the Péronne bridgehead and ordered Heeresgruppe Rupprecht to retake Hallu by counterattack.

Haig and Foch conferred during the morning of 10 August to discuss the situation. Although both agreed to extend the strategic attack by ordering the British Third Army to advance on Bapaume, Haig was less enthusiastic to follow Foch's intent to continue the advance of the Fourth Army to the Somme as he did not share Foch's assessment that the German Second Army was now thoroughly demoralized. However, in the belief that further advances were possible he agreed that the Fourth Army too would continue its offensive.

Rawlinson's view of the battle situation was similar to Kuhl's. The events of the day had made him acutely aware that the scales of advantage were shifting as only 38 tanks remained fit for action and his artillery had not yet located the new German battery positions. However, he did not raise any specific objections to his orders and passed them on to his subordinates. Haig began to gain a clearer view of the situation in the afternoon when he visited the HQs of both the Canadian Corps and 32nd Division, where both Currie and Lambert impressed upon him the tougher resistance their troops were now encountering.

11 AUGUST 1918

For the renewed assault on Lihons, 1st Australian Division retained the 2nd and 3rd Australian brigades in the front line; however, the reserve battalions in each formation relieved those that had fought the previous day. Six tanks from the 2nd Tank Battalion were to support the attack in addition to a heavy artillery barrage.

The final preparations were hindered by the dark and the proximity of an alert enemy, causing the tanks to arrive late and miss H-Hour. However, a thick mist rose and covered the Australians as they moved forwards. To the right, the 7th and 8th Australian battalions worked their way forwards south of Lihons striking into the left flank of 5th Bavarian Division and the right flank of 38th Division. Blinded by the mist, the defenders fired wildly at the

Oberstleutnant Erich Löwenhardt. Löwenhardt was the third highest scoring German ace of the war with 54 'kills' to his credit. He was a ruthless and skilled air fighter who made a formidable opponent in the Fokker DVII, scoring 24 victories in June and July 1918. He was killed in the fierce air fighting over the Somme on 10 August when he collided with an inexperienced wingman immediately after he claimed a SE5a as his final victim. Although both pilots escaped from their crippled aircraft, Löwenhardt's parachute failed to open and he fell to his death.

Australians who picked off each position in turn. The conditions continued to cause confusion as heavy firing could be heard to the rear. Patrols were sent to investigate, and discovered that the 3rd Australian Brigade had started off from the western, rather than the eastern, edge of Crépey Wood and had been subsequently delayed. Swinging around to the north of Lihons, 3rd Australian Brigade caught II/19th and III/21st Bavarian infantry regiments by surprise and drove them back. Between 0600hrs and 0800hrs, both brigades tightened their grip on their objectives by clearing up the remaining isolated defenders and establishing contact with troops on either flank.

As the mist cleared, the Australians found themselves in a commanding position overlooking the old 1916 battlefield. The expected counterattacks were not long in coming and at 0845hrs I and III/19th Bavarian Infantry Regiment advanced on Crépey Wood whilst II/21st Bavarian Infantry Regiment attacked Lihons. They were met by heavy machine-gun fire, however, and halted on the Framerville–Lihons road. To the south the efforts of the 38th Division muddled through a welter of conflicting orders and counter-orders. First ordered to attack the Canadians in Hallu at 0630hrs, their objective was changed to Lihons after the Australian attack. The change of objective was cancelled then quickly reinstated by LI Corps, this time to attack in conjunction with the 21st Division advancing south from Vermandovillers. This order was refined at 0750hrs with the 38th Division directed to wait until the 21st Division's attack took effect before moving off. In an increasingly exasperated state, at 0908hrs the commander of 38th Division ordered his men to attack regardless. At 0930hrs II/96th Infantry Regiment attacked but was stopped by artillery fire on the Chilly–Lihons road. At 1300hrs II/96th Infantry Regiment tried again, this time with I/96th Infantry Regiment and some artillery in support, but again no headway could be made. A final attack was made at 1630hrs which closed right up to the Australian front line, but at this critical juncture many of the key German junior commanders were wounded or killed and the assault was subsequently driven back.

The 5th and 7th Australian brigades delivered the 2nd Australian Division attack, each supported by two brigades of field artillery but without any

Men of the 6th (Victoria) Battalion in trenches in front of Lihons on 10 August. The two soldiers in the centre of the picture are showing off two Luger pistols 'souvenired' from the battlefield. (IWM E (Aus) 2867)

tanks. The barrage was effective and in conjunction with the mist greatly facilitated the Australian assault. On the right 7th Australian Brigade met little resistance and secured its objective with ease. The 5th Australian Brigade on the left had a tougher fight. The remnants of 232nd, 227th and 52nd infantry regiments, on the left flank of the 107th Division, withdrew as the Australians moved forwards, covering their movement with machine-gun fire. Heavy casualties were sustained amongst the company and platoon leaders, but by 0800hrs the Australians were digging in on their objectives except on the extreme left flank along the Roman road. After the mist lifted they spent the remainder of the day under heavy sniper and machine-gun fire, which continued until evening.

In 3rd Australian Division's sector, Major-General Gellibrand ordered 11th Australian Brigade to seize the now-exposed Méricourt Spur in the evening. At 2030hrs the 41st Australian Battalion advanced along a 'corridor' formed between two standing artillery barrages. The 108th Division had intended to withdraw their troops from this exposed position in the coming night but now found themselves pre-empted. After hard fighting with several posts of the 97th and 13th infantry regiments, the 41st (Queensland) Battalion reached the Somme, cutting off the remaining Germans on the spur and taking 300 prisoners.

The 13th Australian Brigade north of the Somme had an anxious day. German guns south of the river fired at the exposed Australian posts with one company of the 50th (South Australia) Battalion sustaining 49 casualties out of a total strength of 110 men. German troops were observed moving into Bray and onto the south-eastern portion of the Etinehem Spur. The Australians braced themselves for a counterattack that never materialized as the Germans were simply reoccupying ground abandoned precipitately the previous night.

In accordance with the directive issued by Fourth Army, Currie ordered the 4th Canadian and 32nd divisions to continue the Canadian Corps' attack at 0420hrs in conjunction with the French First Army on the right. However, following difficulties in getting the tank support forwards in time the attack was delayed until 0930hrs. A breakdown in communication with the French

German troops undergoing assault training in 1918 using a trench to move forwards similarly to the 38th Division at Lihons. Most have slung their rifles and wear improvised 'waistcoats' that hold a supply of hand grenades. (IWM Q 45341)

11 August 1918, holding the Line

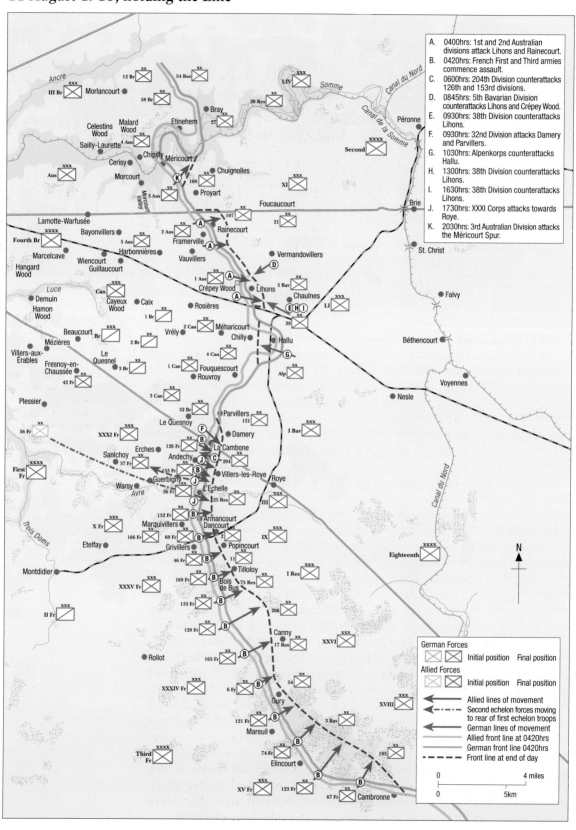

A. 0400hrs: 1st and 2nd Australian divisions attack Lihons and Rainecourt.
B. 0420hrs: French First and Third armies commence assault.
C. 0600hrs: 204th Division counterattacks 126th and 153rd divisions.
D. 0845hrs: 5th Bavarian Division counterattacks Lihons and Crépey Wood.
E. 0930hrs: 38th Division counterattacks Lihons.
F. 0930hrs: 32nd Division attacks Damery and Parvillers.
G. 1030hrs: Alpenkorps counterattacks Hallu.
H. 1300hrs: 38th Division counterattacks Lihons.
I. 1630hrs: 38th Division counterattacks Lihons.
J. 1730hrs: XXXI Corps attacks towards Roye.
K. 2030hrs: 3rd Australian Division attacks the Méricourt Spur.

German Forces

⊠	⊠	
Initial position	Final position	

Allied Forces

⊠	⊠	
Initial position	Final position	

Allied lines of movement
Second echelon forces moving to rear of first echelon troops
German lines of movement
Allied front line at 0420hrs
German front line 0420hrs
Front line at end of day

0 — 4 miles
0 — 5km

N

126th Division on the right prevented this delay being passed on and as a result the French attacked at 0420hrs as planned.

The 32nd Division planned to fire a heavy artillery barrage on the strongpoints of Damery and Parvillers to enable the 14th Brigade to envelop them from north and south and attack from the flank and rear. Unfortunately, the attack misfired from the outset. As a result of the rolling barrage being placed 500 instead of 300 yards ahead of the infantry and a lack of French support on the right flank, the 204th and 121st divisions were able to fire unhindered into the British tanks and infantry. Twelve out of 16 tanks in support were rapidly knocked out. At 1100hrs two tanks managed to enter Damery; however, the infantry being pinned down outside the village were unable to follow up and secure the village. Parvillers remained inviolate, secure behind the strong trench and wire defences of the 1916 battle. At 1005hrs Lambert was instructed not to press his assault if it would result in heavy casualties and he immediately passed orders to the attacking troops to hold their reserves back. At 1230hrs he received further instructions to consolidate the ground now held.

The 4th Canadian Division found that their plan to advance was pre-empted by the newly arrived Alpenkorps, who launched their own counterattack to retake Hallu and Chilly. As the 10th and 12th Canadian brigades waited to advance they came under heavy artillery fire, which by 1000hrs had developed into a full barrage. The right-hand assault was delivered at 1030hrs by the Leib Infantry Regiment, which had been reinforced with I/60 and I/56 Reserve infantry regiments from 121st Division. Although they sustained severe casualties they pushed the 50th Canadian Battalion back from the southern side of Hallu. The 78th (Winnipeg Grenadiers) Battalion hung on until 1300hrs; however, facing an increasingly untenable position it withdrew to the main line of defence east of Chilly. The left-hand assault was intended to be delivered by 1st Jäger Regiment, but owing to the late arrival of the orders to the companies in the line, their attack was never delivered less the covering of the left flank of the Lieb Infantry Regiment. At 1800hrs further attempts to attack Chilly were cancelled.

Canadian infantry and a Mk. V tank cooperate to destroy a machine-gun position along the Amiens–Chaulnes railway near Lihons. The machine gun being hunted is situated beyond the railway in the Australian sector whilst the Canadian troops in view are under long-range machine-gun fire from their right. (IWM E (Aus) 2881)

The attack in the French sector ran out of steam on 11 August. In the First Army, XXXI Corps attacked at dawn with the 126th Division making little headway against the 204th Division now in place in Villers-les-Roye. Indeed a counterattack by 204th Division drove both 126th and 153rd divisions a short distance back. Having relieved 37th Division with 56th Division, Toulorge launched a final assault at 1730hrs but, despite a small advance, his tired troops could push no farther and came to a halt 4km short of Roye. X Corps forced 25th Division out of Armancourt at 1100hrs but two subsequent assaults on Dancourt and Popincourt proved fruitless. XXXV Corps worked its way doggedly through the old trench systems in the Bois de Bus and the Parc de Tilloloy before finally coming to rest on the western outskirts of Tilloloy Village.

Humbert ordered the Third Army to drive forwards towards Noyon, but his attack did little more than push back the rearguards of the Eighteenth Army. XXXIV Corps advanced as far as Canny and Gury, whilst XV Corps cleared the defensive positions around Mareuil and Elincourt before halting. Haig spent the morning visiting the HQs of the Australian and III Corps, where Lieutenant-General Godley from XXII Corps had relieved the exhausted Butler. He received evidence that the offensive power of the Fourth Army was now spent and that the resistance of the defenders was markedly improved. Following a meeting with Rawlinson at Villers-Bretonneux he ordered the offensive to be stopped until the Fourth Army could regroup for a formal attack on the new German positions to be delivered on 14 or 15 August. General Byng visited Haig during his travels in the day and was instructed to now launch the Third Army into the attack against Bapaume as soon as he received reinforcement in order to outflank the positions south of the Somme.

On the French front, Debeney ordered a continuation of the offensive the following day at 1930hrs. However, at 2330hrs, after considering the lack of British support on his left, he postponed the attack until further preparations could be carried out.

Despite Foch's urgings the assault of the Fourth Army did not materialize until three days later. The original timeframe was wildly optimistic as the crucial components of Rawlinson's armoury had lost their strength, in particular the artillery, which had insufficient time to locate the German gun positions to mount an effective counterbattery strike. Likewise the Tank Corps, which had but a handful of tanks fit for action, could not recuperate in such a short period. Consequently the battle of Amiens drew to a close.

AFTERMATH

Although major offensive operations at Amiens halted on 11 August, the effects of the battle were far reaching. The weight of the Allied blow clearly demonstrated the cracking morale of the German fighting troops. The Germans reported losing 27,000 casualties on 8 August, and 33,000 casualties overall, out of 48,000 men fielded by the Second and Eighteenth armies between 1 and 10 August. This included the staggering total of 29,873 prisoners, clearly indicating the loss of combat motivation within the front-line divisions. In addition to the human casualties, the British and French captured 499 guns.

The German high command discussed the situation at two conferences held at Spa on 13 and 14 August. Ludendorff displayed the strain he was under by making a wholly unrealistic assessment of the strategic situation. He continued his earlier arguments that others were to blame by remonstrating against the lack of support from the homeland for the war effort and the corrosive effect this was having on the troops. Furthermore,

General Haig congratulating troops of the Canadian Corps in the field at Amiens. Unlike earlier battles, Haig's command style at Amiens involved daily visits to the army, corps and divisional HQs in order to maintain as accurate a picture as possible of the fighting. (IWM CO 3014)

ignoring the evidence of the catastrophic defeat suffered by his forces, he went on to state his belief that the Allies' will to continue fighting could still be worn down by defensive operations. Despite reports that the Kaiser instigated a diplomatic effort for peace via the queen of the Netherlands during a Crown Council on 14 August, little activity seems to have subsequently taken place.

The institutional blindness of the imperial court was not matched in the other capitals of the Central Powers. Previous crises in Eastern Europe had been met by transfer of German troops from the Western Front to stabilize the situation. The nature of the defeat at Amiens clearly illustrated that this support would no longer be forthcoming. An appeal to the Germans by the Austrian emperor for an immediate armistice was curtly rebuffed on 14 August and again on 14 September. The following day saw the Allies open the battle of Monastir-Doiran in Macedonia, which shattered the Bulgarian Army. On 26 September the Bulgarians requested an armistice.

The battle of Amiens was followed by a succession of blows as the Allies struck all along the Western Front, executing Foch's strategy in what became know as the '100 Day Campaign'. Byng's Third Army launched the battle of Albert on 21 August and eight days later was in possession of Bapaume. Haig continued to expand his attacks to the north as he brought Horne's First Army, containing the recently transferred Canadian Corps, into action on 26 August at Arras. Ludendorff's belated agreement to withdraw to a 'winter line' on the Somme in response was too little too late. His troops found themselves harried by numerous small-scale actions as they were bounced from the Somme position by the enterprising Australians at Mont St Quentin. By 10 September they were back in the Hindenburg Line nervously awaiting the next Allied move. At the forefront of these efforts was the Fourth Army, buoyed by their success at Amiens and confident in their tactical dominance of the battlefield.

The progress of the campaign during August encouraged Haig and Foch to develop plans for a general offensive with a view to ending the war in 1918. Together they envisaged a massive synchronized attack stretching from the Meuse to Ypres with a view to shattering the German positions. On 26, 27, 28 and 29 September the French, American, British and Belgian Armies launched a series of coordinated assaults, which cleared both the Ypres and St Mihiel salients, and shattered the once impregnable Hindenburg Line in a matter of days.

The breaking of the Hindenburg Line finally opened the eyes of the German High Command. The general offensive coincided with the capitulation of their Bulgarian allies, causing Ludendorff to suffer a fit. On 29 September he finally admitted that his army was beaten and that an armistice should be requested in order to save it from total destruction. During the last six weeks of the war the Allies maintained their pressure on Germany, with a series of assaults that crossed the rivers Selle and Sambre, and culminated on the Franco-Belgian border on 11 November.

THE BATTLEFIELD TODAY

The battlefield at Amiens is among the best preserved on the Western Front. Although the A1 and A29 autoroutes cross the battlefield, their impact is minimal. Agriculture remains the mainstay of the local economy and relatively little urban development has taken place in the intervening period. Some of the woods that played such a significant part in the battle, such as the Bois du Dé and Celestins Wood, have since been cut down; however, their locations can easily be found by comparing modern IGN maps with those used in 1918. On the whole the villages retain their 1918 boundaries, which give a good impression of the approaches and fields of fire available to attacker and defender alike.

The battlefield is large, being over 50km broad from Cambronne on the Oise to Dernancourt on the Somme, and approximately 20km deep from Villers-Bretonneux to the Lihons–Hallu area. A vehicle is therefore essential to visit the whole front of the attack. However, traffic is light away from the main roads and, despite being so close to the 1916 Somme battlefield, the Amiens battlefield possesses a far less 'claustrophobic' atmosphere. It lacks the formally developed sites and receives far fewer visitors than its northern neighbour. Consequently, exploration by foot or bicycle at a more local level gives an excellent opportunity to reflect on the events of 1918 and is essential to get a true feel for the terrain, particularly in the Somme and Avre valleys.

In modern parlance the battle of Amiens was the first truly joint (air/land) and combined (multinational) operation of the 20th century and was a stunning success for the Allies. It should be remembered as such.

BIBLIOGRAPHY

Barnett, C., *The Swordbearers: Supreme Command in The First World War,* Cassell: London, 2000

Bean, C. E. W., *Official History of Australia in the Great War, Vol VI, The AIF in France 1918,* Angus and Robertson: Sydney, 1942

Bose, T. von, *Schlachten des Weltkrieges, Die Katastrophe des 8 August 1918,* Stalling: Oldenburg, 1930

Childs, David J., *A Peripheral Weapon? The Production and Employment of British Tanks in the First World War,* Greenwood Press: London, 1999

Crow, Duncan, *Armoured Fighting Vehicles of the World, Vol I,* Profile Publications: Windsor, 1970

Daille, M., *La Bataille de Montdidier,* Berger-Levrault: Paris, 1924

Der Weltkrieg 1914-1918: die militärischen operationen zu lande, Vol 14, Die Kriegführung an der Westfront im Jahre 1918, Mittler und Sohn: Berlin, 1944

Die Bayern im Grossen Kriege 1914–1918 Bayerischen Kreigsarchiv: Munich, 1923

Edmonds, J. E., *History of the Great War, Military Operations France and Belgium 1918, Vol IV, 8th August–26th September, The Franco-British Offensive* Battery Press: Nashville, 1993

Grasset, A., *Montdidier: Le 8 Aout 1918 à la 42e Division,* Berger-Levrault: Paris, 1930

Harris, J. P., *Amiens to the Armistice,* Brassey: London, 1998

Harris, J. P., *Men, Ideas and Tanks: British Military Thought and Armoured Forces, 1903–1939,* Manchester University Press: Manchester, 1995

Jones, H. A., *The War in the Air, Vol VI,* Oxford University Press: Oxford, 1937

Les Armées Françaises dans La Grande Guerre, Tome VII, Ier Vol, Imprimerie Nationale: Paris, 1923

McWilliams, J., and Steel, R. J., *Amiens 1918* Tempus: Stroud, 2004

Nicholson, G. W. L., *Canadian Expeditionary Force 1914–1919: Official History of the Canadian Army in the Great War* Roger Duhamel: Ottawa, 1962

Prior, R., and Wilson, T., *Command on the Western Front: The Military Career of Sir Henry Rawlinson 1914–1918* Leo Cooper: Barnsley, 2004

Sheffield, G., and Bourne, J., *Douglas Haig: War Diaries and Letters 1914–1918* Weidenfeld and Nicholson: London, 2005

Van Wyngarden, G., Aviation Elite Units 16: *Richthofen's Circus: Jagdgeschwader Nr I,* Osprey Publishing Ltd: Oxford, 2004

Van Wyngarden, G., Aviation Elite Units 19: *Jagdgeschwader Nr II: Geschwader 'Berthold',* Osprey Publishing Ltd: Oxford, 2005

Votaw, J. F., Battle Orders 6: *The American Expeditionary Forces in World War I,* Osprey Publishing Ltd: Oxford, 2005

INDEX